THE BOOK OF PATAGONIA

Its History from Magellan to our days

JUAN MANUEL HERRERA TRAYBEL

Herrera Traybel, Juan Manuel
 The book of Patagonia : Its History from Magellan to our days / Juan Manuel
Herrera Traybel. - 1a ed. - Ciudad Autónoma de Buenos Aires : Juan Manuel Herrera
Traybel, 2022.
 282 p. ; 23 x 15 cm.

 ISBN 978-987-88-4132-8

 1. Historia. 2. Patagonia. 3. Historia Argentina. I. Título.
 CDD 982

Cover photo: courtesy from Ángel Adaro.

DEDICATION

To my parents, Francisco and Laura.

CONTENTS

ACKNOWLEDGMENTS

To Margit and her family for their patience and support during this process. To Christian and Sabine Frei who pushed me to start writing this book. To my teachers Carlos Balboa Fernandez and Claudio Bertonatti who also helped me to find this path.

To Juan Pablo "Raptor" Raposo, Ángel Adaro, Luis Quezada, Ignacio Canepa and Laura Devoto for their photographic contribution.

Gustavo del Valle, Gustavo Sebastián, Nazarena Paschetta for their constructive criticism. Ángel Andres Subirá López for his historical contribution about the area of Gobernador Gregores.

Martín "Doc" Canale and Fernando Coronato for their review on the Welsh colony in Chubut. Carlos Vairo and his contribution as director of the Ushuaia Maritime Museum. To the Archivo Visual Patagonico. To Estancia Cristina Sociedad Anónima for the access to the material and for being the inspiration and facilitator of this new facet in my life.

PREFACE

Patagonia is a large geographical region in South America shared by Argentina and Chile, with the Andes Mountains in between. The name itself evokes adventure. It is a land of explorers, of nature and sublime landscapes, of those that dwarf the soul of those who are lucky enough to visit this region. The name Patagonia is a seed. The superlative images of its majestic landscapes are like drops of water that encourage the desire to get to know this region.

At first, Patagonia is seen through the eyes: the mountains, the lakes, the glaciers, the green forests and the vast steppe. Then the rest of the senses make their experience at the same time: the wind, the cold, the dryness. We realise that we are far away from everything: from the facilities of a big city, from the everyday comfort, from the closeness to the usual. In the end you discover that you are surrounded by a immense, fragile yet beautiful wilderness.

Human beings have known Patagonia since before it was called Patagonia. And I would imagine that the experience back then would have been no different. The region, with its geographical and climatic characteristics, has always been a hostile, immense, precarious, solitary environment. The environment seems to resist humans adapting to it. This book will attempt to tell the story of human adaptation to this region from its beginnings to the present day.

After living in Patagonia several years, i felt that those who inhabited this region deserve special consideration.

Working with the National Parks in the Argentinean side of Patagonia, I was able to experience firsthand these beautiful and isolated landscapes. Later, when I got in touch with the history of the place, I realized that knowing the events that took place in this region gave more meaning to the experience of being here. Knowing these facts completed the puzzle that formed the different images we know about Patagonia. And so, by investigating, it awakened my curiosity. Curiosity that will turn me into the curator of a museum in Patagonia just a few years later.

My historical analysis cannot be considered academic, as I have neither the formal qualifications nor the studies necessary to make such a claim. What I can offer is the result of a historical compilation based on the curiosity of the seven intense years I lived in the region and which, unwittingly, led me to work in a museum putting a forgotten story together.

The work that follows is inspired by my time as curator of a museum in a Patagonian Estancia, and will serve to give you a general idea of the different events that formed part of the history of Patagonia today. The reader, therefore, should discard any preconceived ideas about the he region and its scenic beauty, because you will see this is not a travel guide.

Thanks to this book, where you see a grandiose landscape, you will now see much more: you will see people, families, cultures and communities that, along with their tragedies, achievements and conflicts, have written the history of this region with blood, sweat and tears.

Patagonia is, in this work, the silent witness and the stage of the different historical events and processes that took place here. The events and contexts I describe are arranged in chronological order for the reader to better interpret the development of the idea I seek to capture in the book you hold in your hands.

CHAPTER 1

A part of Gondwana

To begin this book on the history of Patagonia, I want to start by laying the foundations of this marvelous territory. In this book, we will discuss the different events that have shaped the present character of the region, taking into account many of the processes that have been happening since the beginning of time.

During my tertiary studies I took Geography, where I learnt that the best way to interpret a territory is to begin by presenting the historical origin of the physical place where the events that we want to revise are taking place. Knowing the setting of the region will highlight each one of the events from this book.

It doesn't matter if you don't know this region yet. What I will describe in this chapter should sound familiar, like the theory of *plate tectonics* and the theory of *human displacement*.

The aim of this chapter is to clarify doubts about the location of the Patagonian region on the present map of the world and its origin, not only anthropological but also geologically. Therefore, in the following lines I will develop this long process in the lightest way possible.

If you wish, you can repeat this chapter several times during the reading of the book.

The plate tectonics theory

Plate tectonics is the theory that Earth's land masses are in constant motion. According to the theory, until 200 million years ago, there was only one supercontinent on planet Earth, which was called "Pangaea". Gradually, this supercontinent split in two, giving birth to "Laurasia" in the north and "Gondwana" in the south.

Located then in the south of the globe, Gondwana was later subdivided into large blocks separated by fractures in the Earth's crust. These new continents or sub-continents, were dispersed originating the actual South America, Africa, Australia, New Zealand, some South Pacific islands, a part of India, and Antarctica. This last process, which has been going on for 200 million years and counting, gave the shape we know of the map of the world and we have summarized it in these brief lines.

That is why I decided to call this chapter "a part of Gondwana" as South America corresponds to a portion of this ancient supercontinent.

Changes on the Earth

South America was very different from what it is today.

Once Gondwana splits from Laurasia, an era known as the Jurassic began. It lasted approximately 55 million years and, in general terms, is a little far from the images we saw in the movie *Jurassic Park*. But the adaptations of species to the new terrain are great. For example: the first frogs appear, and most of the dinosaurs that evolve at the beginning are herbivores. Flying reptiles will also appear here, but the famous predators of the film did not appear in this time period.

At the end of the Jurassic period, 145 million years ago, the subdivision of Gondwana began.

In this new era, called the Cretaceous, dinosaurs dominated the terrain while rodents scurried at their feet through forests of ferns, cycads and conifers. Now we can say that the famous velociraptors and the T-Rex appeared before they've become Hollywood stars.

At the end of the Cretaceous period 70 million years ago, the oceans filled in the gaps that separated the isolated continents, which were already shaped much like today. Flowering plants spread across the landscape. And mammals settled in, ready to fill the void soon left by the extinct dinosaurs.

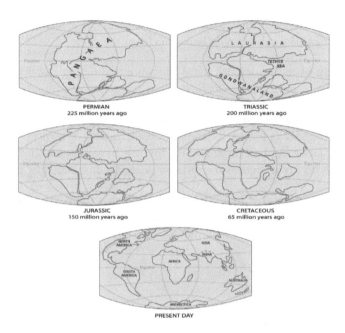

The breakup of Pangaea and motion of their continents to their present-day positions
*Credit: U.S. Geological Survey, Department of the Interior/USGS / U.S. Geological
Survey/photo by Kious, Jacquelyne; Tilling, Robert I.; Kiger, Martha, Russel, Jane
Wikimedia Commons - Public Domain*

The new era: 65 million years ago

Before speaking of Patagonia dominated by the steppe, and characterized by the Andes mountain-range (also known as *Cordillera de los Andes* or just *Cordillera*), we must imagine that the mountain range did not exist. Also, the climate was warmer, and this allowed the development of large animals or *mega-fauna* and extensive coniferous forests.

Whether or not an asteroid caused the extinction of more than half of the planet's species at the end of the Cretaceous is still a matter of scientific debate. But shifting continents, widening coastlines and oceans cooling the planet's climate, caused major changes in the planet's fauna and flora. At this time of huge changes, the Earth would have been so vulnerable, that a cataclysm the size of an asteroid or a period of internal volcanic activity would have marked the end of the Cretaceous.

This cataclysm took with it a biodiversity that we are now reconstructing piece by piece with the various discoveries being made on the planet.

The origin of the Andes and the Alpine mountain-range provide evidence that shifting in the tectonic plates may have brought a period of darkness and vulcanism.

After the continents shifted, the Andes appeared and the geography changed and this gave Patagonia ts present configuration. As further evidence, petrified forests (Sarmiento, Jaramillo, La Leona) and the findings of the largest dinosaurs that inhabited this planet are in sight. Patagonia was a region dominated by giants long ago.

Talking about the mountains, the most emblematic ones are Mount Fitz Roy, Cerro Torre and the Torres del Paine. Although they are part of the Patagonian Andes, their final shape was acquired after the different glacial periods took place on earth.

The wind and the actual Patagonian landscape

Many of you know Patagonia thanks to its mountains, lakes and glaciers decorated by green forests and accompanied by exquisite fauna. But this Patagonia of lakes, forests and mountains covers only 10% of its total territory. The remaining 90% corresponds to a steppe landscape, a semi-desert where shrubs and hard grasses abound. These two opposed environments like the forest and the deserts are born thanks to one fundamental factor: the influence of the oceanic wind.

Patagonia is a geographic region comprising the territories of Argentina and Chile extending from 40° south latitude to Cape Horn. The influence of the Atlantic wind ceases to have its effect on the Pampa and, from approximately the parallel 40 of south latitude towards the south, the influence of the Pacific wind begins to give shape to this region.

The *Roaring Forties* are a system of winds that cross the Pacific Ocean from West to East. After passing by Australia and New Zealand, the wind travels across the Pacific and carry moisture to the Andes Mountains in Patagonia. The south of South America (Patagonia) is the first continental mass that these winds encounter and on which they discharge their humidity, providing the Andes Mountains with ice, snow and forests.

The accumulation of snow and ice is so big that the Southern Patagonian Ice Field was born in between the Andes: this is the third largest mass of ice of the world after Antarctica and Greenland.

The native forest is normally surrounding the Andes range and is dominated by a family of trees that date back to the time of the dinosaur. The forest of Patagonia is home to the family of false beeches or *Nothofagus*. Their distribution in the world is limited to the southern hemisphere, as they were formed in Gondwana. Such trees can be found also in Australia, or New Zealand. These forests are home to many animals and birds that visit this region, but once again, it only occupies 10% of the entire Patagonian territory.

Astronaut photograph ISS038-E-47324 was acquired on February 13, 2014, with a Nikon D3S digital camera using a 65 millimeter lens, and is provided by the ISS Crew Earth Observations Facility and the Earth Science and Remote Sensing Unit, Johnson Space Center. The image was taken by the Expedition 38 crew. It has been cropped and enhanced to improve contrast, and lens artifacts have been removed. The International Space Station Program supports the laboratory as part of the ISS National Lab to help astronauts take pictures of Earth that will be of the greatest value to scientists and the public, and to make those images freely available on the Internet. Additional images taken by astronauts and cosmonauts can be viewed at the NASA/JSC Gateway to Astronaut Photography of Earth. Caption by M. Justin Wilkinson, Jacobs at NASA-JSC. The author added the references.

The winds from the Pacific dump almost all its moisture in the Andean zone, leaving little or nothing for the remaining areas of Patagonia, which extends eastwards for almost 300 kilometers to the Atlantic Ocean: this is how the Patagonian steppe is born.

The Patagonian steppe, although at first glance it seems unattractive, is home to many species of great scientific interest, and was also suitable terrain for the anthropological development of the region.

Now that we have defined the terrain, let's talk about who populated, in this case, the American continent.

The Bering Land Bridge Theory

This is a theory that still has a strong consensus today and speaks of the crossing of ethnic groups from Siberia to North America across the Bering Strait in the last glacial period around 20,000 years ago.

The theory holds that when the last Ice Age took place, the sea level dropped abruptly, leaving land clear of the water that usually covers it. The Bering Strait has a current depth between 30 to 50 meters, and it is estimated that people from Siberia crossed it from Siberia to North America. According to experts, this water-free passage existed for several thousand years, making it possible for ethnic groups from Siberia to cross into the actual American continent. Today the theory is in crisis due to new genetic studies, perhaps in a few years we will have other certainties, or perhaps they will end up confirming this approach.

The advance of settlers in the new continent seems, at first glance, to be gradual, with the oldest cultures of the American continent in the north of the continent and slowly settling in Central and South America. Although there are many findings that do not match in time with this theory, for the time being it is still the strongest theory.

In today's southern Patagonia

Magellan's encounter with the natives of the region in 1520, and many archeological and anthropological findings, put the original inhabitants of South America on the map at least 12,000 years ago.

In Argentina, in the province of Santa Cruz to be precise, is the so-called *Cueva de las Manos* (Cave of the Hands). It is an incredible place that I was lucky enough to visit. Its interest lies in the beauty of the cave paintings, as well as in its antiquity: so far, the oldest inscriptions date back to about 9,300 years ago. It is one of the oldest artistic expressions of South American peoples. This place has been designated a National Historic Monument and declared a World Heritage Site by United Nations.

Cave paintings are one of the most important and valuable archeological remains, because it not only provides information about the human activities of these past societies, but also about their way of seeing the world through artistic expressions.

Along with the native peoples, species coexisted for thousands of years and accompanied the development of life in this part of the Earth. On the continent, the puma, the guanaco, the *choique* and other smaller animals stand out.

Cave paintings of hands and guanacos in Cueva de las Manos.
Photo: "Guanacos ancestrales" by Viajar Ahora is under license CC BY 2.0

Aboriginal peoples: Mapuche and Tehuelche

In the current province of Santa Cruz and the last part of continental America, the presence of the Tehuelche people stood out. They had been called *Patagones* by European sailors and gave their name to this territory as the basis for the myth of their gigantism. The origins of these people can be traced in archeological sites that show very similar patterns of technology, diet and housing models called *tolderías* (constructions with wood and guanaco skins tied with *choique* tendons).

Two phases can be distinguished in its cultural development. The first phase was documented by the references of some European travelers. At first, they were divided into nomadic groups on foot, dedicated to hunting guanaco (a llama-related camelid) and *choique* (a flightless small ostrich), as well as gathering coastal products. They used bows and arrows and spears.

In the next phase they adopted the horse brought from Europe, an animal that changed their way of life. These horses would have escaped or been abandoned by settlers during the 16th century, and being in a very favorable environment, they would have reproduced and spread throughout Patagonia. The main consequence of the adoption of the horse was a significant increase in the distances traveled, making contact with neighboring populations more frequent.

With the settlement of the white man in this territory, they began to do business with them. Sometimes attacks to small populations were reported and their reputation in the Argentine capital was not positive.

You can also find the Mapuche people, originally from Chile. The Mapuche (people of the land, in their language) are also one of the most important aboriginal groups in Patagonia.

They were gatherers and hunters, but one of their most relevant features is the importance they gave to language and literature as a way of preserving their identity.

Their subsistence was based on hunting guanaco and choique; they also gathered roots and seeds from which they made flour. They practiced nomadism between the plateau and the Pacific coast. On the coast they gathered shellfish and hunted marine mammals. They worked leather with stone tools and made boats, blankets, clothing and even built their dwellings. These were also *toldos*, divided into two compartments, one for men and the other for women and children.

The Mapuche had their own calendar, which still governs some of their festivals today. The Mapuches are currently active in land claims in different parts of Patagonia.

The current situation of indigenous peoples:

Unfortunately, their numbers have dwindled considerably, and while some reserves are trying to maintain their language and customs, the presence of the culture is almost extinct. Attempts are now being made to rename places with their aboriginal nomenclature to vindicate those who once roamed these vast extensions of virgin land.

For example, the province of Santa Cruz offers a ton of archeological and anthropological evidence. This helps even more to understand the way of life and cosmovision of the Tehuelches, who were subdued by the arrival of Europeans.

Today there is a dam project on the Santa Cruz River that endangers many of these archeological sites. These sites are mostly near the river and these areas will be flooded after this project.

Hopefully the authorities will review the situation before such a project is carried out, and even more so I hope that the project does not take place at all. Although at this time the works are going ahead despite several complaints against them.

Summary

In this chapter we have been able to locate South America on the map, quickly seeing how the current configuration of this continent was formed, and we have seen how life found its way here. We saw how the animal and plant species that lived in the territory evolved and how recent events in earth's history changed its shape forever. After this, we were able to locate the arrival of the homo-sapiens on this continent in order to understand his migration to this new continent and how those who settled in Patagonia lived.

CHAPTER 2

The settlement of Patagonia

In this chapter we are going to learn about how the settlement of Patagonia took shape, talking about human beings and their relationship with the environment. The idea is to understand the characteristics of the first settlers who arrived in this remote area, and then we will describe the best-known native peoples of Argentine Patagonia.

We often speak of Patagonia as the *"End of the World"* and we think about how isolated this corner of the planet is, only separated from Antarctica by mere 1,000 kilometers.

It is normal to relate this nickname to the hostilities of the climate, the remoteness, the lack of resources, and the challenges this brings.

We will discuss now not only human settlement, but also how plants and animals got settled here as well and i will try to be as practical as possible in this chapter too. I do not want to train experts in the field, but to give the most practical details as possible. My aim is for the reader to understand why Patagonia is the way it is. I also want to make clear that the theories I use are among the most widely accepted at present, and those which I think, to the best of my knowledge, are those which allowed the development of the processes that formed the region.

Profile of the new settlers

Anatomically modern men *(homo sapiens)*, according to the African theory, appeared approximately 200,000 years ago and began to spread throughout the Middle East, Europe, South Asia and Siberia. As what matters to me is that the reader understands the process that took place in South America, I avoid giving further details on dates.

One key event is the last Ice Age, which took place some 20,000 years ago. At that time, the Earth experienced the maximum advance of ice, with incalculable glacial densities that, according to experts, lowered sea levels by more than 100 meters. Thanks to this event, a wide strip of ocean between today's Russia and the United States was uncovered for several thousand years and allowed humans living on the Siberian steppes to reach a new continent: America. This is the famous Bering Land Bridge route.

The Bering Strait theory is really interesting as the actual depth of the Bering Strait, and the great breadth of this not-so-deep seabed, could have allowed during the last Ice Age the passage of men from one continent to another.

Now, anatomically modern humans arrived in America and began to move slowly from the North to the South of America.

These groups will continue to colonize new lands for millennia, and so they will conquer new terrains. Just imagining these groups in these times crossing the Great Plains of the United States, colonizing present-day Costa Rica or venturing into the Amazon is simply fascinating.

These journeys across such difficult terrains demonstrate that the peoples who arrived in South America brought with them a lot of experience. Experience in exploration, adaptation and survival, as they have already walked for several hundred years in terrains with different characteristics and challenges. These groups had enormous technological sophistication and had undergone a variety of adaptive experiences that prepared them to successfully occupy any type of environment.

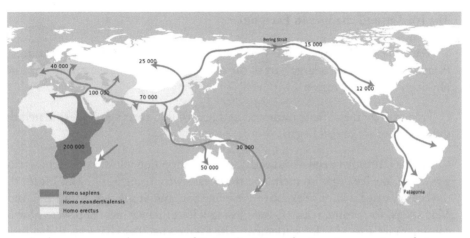

In the map we see the crossing of Bering Strait into the American continent, being
Patagonia the end of the journey.
*De NordNordWest - Spreading homo sapiens ru.svg by Urutseg which based on Spreading homo
sapiens.jpg by Altaileopard. Public Domain*

Patagonia before the arrival of *homo sapiens*

Since we accepted that the populations came from the north to the south, we
will now talk a little about what the Patagonian landscape was like and who lived in
this region before their arrival. For example, Patagonia was inhabited by a mastodon
that reached a height of three meters. There were also panthers and pumas, as well as
guanacoes (llama family) and *huemul* (Andean deer). Except for the mastodon and
the panther that became extinct in this period due to climatic changes, the rest were
able to adapt and became the species that still inhabit Patagonia today.

The famous *mylodon* also lived in Patagonia. It is "famous" because in the 19th
Century, the evidence suggested that there were still specimens living in the dense
Patagonian forests. The mylodon was a kind of giant sloth, which moved slowly and
had a protective shell but went extinct several thousand years ago.

When the last Ice Age was already in decline, these giant species disappeared, and
their disappearance coincides with this time of great changes.

Can you imagine these animals roaming in modern-day Patagonia?

The Ice Age and changes in Patagonia

With the last Ice Age, there were great changes in the geographical aspect of Patagonia. Ice covered a large part of the territory, giving, over the millennia, a new physiognomy to the region.

Progressively the climate improved and just 14,000 years ago it is estimated that the process of ice retreat began.

We have already talked about the water level dropping. Now, as the temperature was rising, the ice began to melt, and the oceans were rising again. This meant that the coastal strips that once existed were being lost, but at the same time, the Andes Mountains, for natural reasons, were losing a lot of its ice mass and were now becoming more accessible for settlement. The ice retreated but changed the landscape leaving large lakes and U-shaped valleys behind. It also shaped mountains and left evidence all over the terrain.

The vegetation of the area remained as it is today, with the cold forests of the Andes Mountains beginning to appear, which are highly adaptable, and the Nothofagus family stands out. Their adaptation is magnificent and some species grow very close to glacial ice. This family of trees dates back to the time of Gondwana and today is distributed throughout most of the southern hemisphere. Due to the extreme conditions of the area, plant diversity is low, but it manages to adapt very well.

In the steppe, which occupies most of the region, the wind begins to predominate and the aridity prevails to this day. In another chapter I will deal with the current landscape and vegetation, talking in more detail about the two predominant environments: Steppe and Forest.

End of the Journey

In these times of great change, and coinciding with the disappearance of the megafauna described above, the arrival of these groups that had been moving down from North America took place. The evidence shows that the hunting of animals in the region dates back approximately 12,000 years, and there is evidence of numerous *huemul* and *guanaco* dating. With the arrival of human beings to this corner of the planet that today we call "the end of the world" this can also be seen as the end of the great journey of human dispersion that began in Africa and ended in Patagonia.

The tribes of Patagonia:

The Tehuelches (Continental Patagonia - Argentina side)

The Tehuelches were the nomadic groups that inhabited the Patagonian steppe. Magellan encountered these groups in his trip, and because of their appearance they called them *"Patagones"*. *Patagon* was the giant in a book called *Primaleon* read by the aristocrats of that time.

These nomads lived by hunting *guanaco* and *choique*. The guanaco is a wild species belonging to the camelid family, related to llamas and alpacas. The choique which is a kind of rhea, but shorter and flightless.

Tehuelches were scattered all over Patagonia, and with the influence of the white man, they adapted to changes such as, for example, the use of the horse. This was a great advance that allowed them to travel great distances.

They lived in tents set up with logs and guanaco skins, called *"tolderías"* or *Kau,* which inside offered comfort on guanaco wool skins that made like a common room that the women during the day use to sew and work the leather for their use. The men were in charge of hunting and in the old days they used the bow and arrow. With the arrival of the Europeans, they began to use spears, *bolas* (a type of throwing weapon made of weights on the ends of interconnected cords, used to capture animals by entangling their legs) and the lasso more frequently.

When the Tehuelche ruled the steppes before the arrival of the Europeans, they buried their dead in the highest and most attractive hills of the plain. In reality, it was not a burial, but they laid the body down and covered it with large stones. This burial place is called a *chenque*.

After the arrival of the Europeans, they began to see how they desecrated the graves for study purposes and began to bury their own in less visible places and prevented any white man from witnessing these burials. Tehuelche communities today are quite small.

27

The Yamana (Insular Patagonia - Tierra del Fuego)

On Tierra del Fuego Island, there was the Yámana or *Yaghan* ethnic group: nomadic groups of canoeists that dominated the sea. They inhabited the beaches of the Beagle Channel and the islands that extend to Cape Horn.

These natives lived naked and covered their bodies with the blubber of marine mammals such as stranded whales or sea lions. Sometimes they wore small sea lion hides. The canoes were made from the bark of trees of the Nothofagus family and always had a fire in them. The women were excellent swimmers and helped maneuver the canoe and procure food, while the men hunted. They used spears and harpoons to kill otters, seals and fish. They moved frequently changing places and the greatest evidence they left behind was the mounds of mussel shells, their main food. The camps consisted of huts made of branches, sticks and grass.

By the time Europeans arrived in the area, there were very few of them and they quickly disappeared for a variety of reasons, one of them being diseases imported into the region by the new visitors.

The Selk'nam (Insular Patagonia - Tierra del Fuego)

The *Selk'nam* (often called Onas) were a larger group of nomads who lived in the interior of Tierra del Fuego Island, mainly following the guanaco. It would be like the adaptation of the Tehuelches to this territory; they also used the bow and arrow for hunting.

They were tall and could track animals with great precision. They did not have access to horses as the Tehuelches did. The guanaco was their main source of food and clothing: they wore their skins with the wool on the outside to cover their entire body and they also produced a kind of shoe with it. They wore this clothing all year round.

Different from the Yámana they never used canoes, spears or harpoons. Fishing was very infrequent and they waited only for low tide. The disappearance of the *Selk'nam* was also very sudden and in this case the emphasis is more on the massacres perpetrated by the white man (which we will mention in a later chapter) than the diseases that came from overseas.

Selk'nam with guanaco clothing items and bows.
Photo: Archivo General de la Nación (1890)

Summary

This was a review of how human beings arrived in Patagonia, and how they adapted to the great changes that occurred during their movement towards the south of the continent. Finally, we've reviewed the most relevant tribes of Argentine Patagonia, and we will mention them again in some of the chapters of this book.

As I said, I tried to explain the processes of human displacement here in the most practical way possible so that you can better understand the journey from the human being to the end of the world.

Lago Anita or Pearson in Estancia Cristina
Photograph kindly shared by Juan Pablo Raposo.

CHAPTER 3

The current landscape

Let us talk about why Patagonia is the way it is. The landscape we know the most are the ones we see in the Patagonia travel advertisements, like the mountains, the forests, the huge lakes and the glaciers. But also, part of the Patagonian scenery is a vast steppe with incredible landscapes like canyons, meandering rivers, and a coastline that ends abruptly at the sea.

To understand the Patagonian landscape, we need to acknowledge that there is an element that we cannot perceive so easily through photographs. That element is the wind.

The wind

The circulation of air with its temperature changes in the atmosphere causes the so-called constant or planetary winds. These winds are the strongest in the southern hemisphere, where our book takes place.

In the southern hemisphere, cold and dense air causes more intense winds. This intensity is mainly due to the displacement of air masses from the Equator towards the poles, and also due to the lack of land masses that can slow down the force of the wind. In other words, the continental mass is greater in the northern hemisphere, so there are more geographical obstacles that hinder the circulation of wind currents. The opposite happens in the southern hemisphere where the lack of landmass leads to more intense wind currents.

The wind belt that affects Patagonia begins at 40° south latitude, and influences all the way south to Cape Horn. This wind blows constantly in the region, imposing the conditions of the vegetation and the landscape.

The Roaring Forties (40°S and southwards)

It should be noted that the South Seas were famous for being the geographical area of exploration for new trade routes, especially by Dutch and English trading companies that operated through the Strait of Magellan or Cape Horn in southern Patagonia. Thus, sailors called this system of constant winds the *Roaring Forties.*

When sailing was still done under sail, these strong and constant winds propelled ships across the Pacific, often at breakneck speed. However, sailing west in rough seas facing strong headwinds could take weeks, especially around Cape Horn, making this place one of the most dangerous sailing passages in the world. Cape Horn also has the highest number of recorded shipwrecks in the world.

These famous constant winds run in a west-easterly (a.k.a. westerlies) direction along the strip from 40° south latitude to the south.

The influence of the wind in Patagonia

The aforementioned winds blow constantly around the world without encountering any obstacles, except for the southern tip of New Zealand on the other side of the globe. The rest is just ocean.

When the wind leaves New Zealand, which I take this opportunity to say is a beautiful country, it begins to cross the great Pacific Ocean that came onto the maps after the voyage of Magellan, who named it that way. On this transoceanic journey, the wind begins collecting moisture. This humid wind moves unchallenged and gradually approaches South America. More precisely, towards the Andes, which awaits the arrival of the cargo brought by the wind.

And at that moment, two great elements of nature collide: the humid wind and an impressive mountain range. The moisture-laden wind begins to gain altitude following the shape of the mountains. As it rises, the wind temperature drops dramatically. And by the time it reaches the top of the mountains this moisture begins to precipitate. A new element appears: water.

The Pacific coast of southern South America, Patagonia, today Chilean territory, receives a large amount of annual rainfall, which makes this beautiful corridor green, originating to one of the most biodiverse areas of the planet, called the Valdivian rainforest. Conifers, Araucarias and many other species decorate this rainforest.

In certain sectors you can find gigantic specimens of one of the longest-living tree species on the planet, the larch tree.

Don't forget that the wind is still blowing and the humidity is still pouring down, but this time over the Andes Mountains. Up there, the precipitation is solid and snow falls for a large part of the year. The amount is impressive, and so much snow falls on the mountains that it feeds one of the largest ice fields in the world: the Southern Patagonian Ice Field. A white blanket of ice of significant density rests protected in the middle of the Andes.

In the mountains, snow also falls in large quantities and favors the formation of glacial ice, which allow Patagonia to have spectacular glaciers that flow like frozen rivers on both sides of the Andes Mountain Range.

But the moisture continues to reach its destination, this time on the other side of the Cordillera in what is now Argentina, with an annual rainfall of up to 2,000 mm, which allows a forest to exist here as well. The forest on the Argentinean side of the mountain range is very narrow. And that is because the wind is already running out of moisture, and the forest starts to fade a few kilometers into the east giving birth to the most extensive ecosystem in the Patagonian region: the steppe.

The steppe is a desert-like plain, where rainfall is around 250 mm per year. It is characterized by hard grasses, thorny bushes and a poorly permeable and extremely dry soil. This environment will be the main place where life will develop, like the life of the Tehuelches that we have already mentioned, and which will later be the setting for some other Patagonian stories that we will relate in this book.

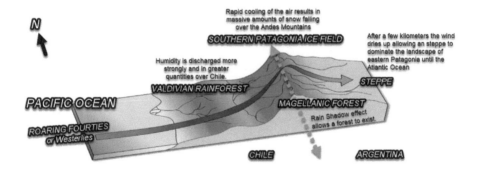

33

The Forest

The Patagonian forest is the sum of the Valdivian rainforest and the Magellanic forest that extends into the Argentinean part of the mountain range.

In the Argentinian sector, there are some parts with a Valdivian Rainforest influence, but for the most part we are talking about a Magellanic forest.

The Magellanic forest is noted for the presence of one of the oldest families of trees on Earth. These trees seemed, at first, to be related to the "beeches" of the genus *Fagus*, well known in the northern hemisphere, but the explorers seem to have confused them with their similarity.

We are talking about the Nothofagus family of trees, its Latin name means "false beech" (*Nothofagus* = Not-a-beech tree). Experts estimate that they appeared in the time of Gondwana, when the Earth undergone great changes and when this supercontinent fragmented, spreading this family throughout the southern hemisphere.

Today there are 40 species in the world, and the Nothofagus inhabit exclusively two continents: Oceania and America.

In my travels, I had the good fortune to visit Australia and New Zealand, where I was able to find Nothofagus specimens. It was a very interesting moment seeing these trees that in another part of the planet. In Australia may be found in places like the Great Otway Ranges and most parts of Tasmania, while in New Zealand only in South Island.

Nothofagus trees at Estancia Cristina.
Photograph kindly shared by Juan Pablo Raposo.

The Steppe

A place that hides nothing, and where you can't hide. You cannot hide from the sun, from the wind, from the cold, from the rain, from the hail. You can't hide from enemies, from dangers, from problems, from destiny.

The Patagonian steppe was inhabited, thousands of years ago, by giant prehistoric animals. This mega-fauna gave way to the current animals of the region, which appeared simultaneously with the arrival of human beings to Patagonia. In these primitive times, life adapted to the demands of the terrain, as well as to the search for food, finding a balance that is reflected in the cave paintings that today bear witness to the early days of man in this region. But with the arrival of the Europeans, everything changed rapidly.

The steppe is an extensive arid plain, which disappears into the horizon or stands out because it may present some elevation. The color is always the same, that yellowish-green tone interspersed with dry sections or hard grasses. In this endless expanse, few mammals and few plant species have managed to adapt to such climatic and competitive challenges. The *Puma* is the top predator that looks for its prey in the guanaco, who move in groups. By chasing after guanaco groups, perhaps one of its members stumbles while trying to escape and will be part of the day's menu. There are also foxes and other animals that complete the list of terrestrial animals. I mention these two animals because they will reappear in this book.

There are steppes in various parts of the world, comparable to the Patagonian Steppe in the central-western United States (Great Basin, in the state of Nevada), and in the semi-desert of Gobi, in Mongolia.

The steppe, the fences and sheep.
Photograph kindly shared by Juan Pablo Raposo.

The climate of today's Patagonian Steppe region has changed drastically, even allowing for the existence of tropical rainforests in ancient times. For example, 144 million years ago, Patagonia was covered with Araucaria forests and populated by dinosaurs, of which there are fossil remains today. Today in Patagonia, petrified forests are well known, as are numerous dinosaur discoveries.

The pressure exerted by the ice that covered the Andes Mountains for thousands of years led to the formation of enormous lakes of glacial origin, which are easily recognizable on a map of the region. Very fertile valleys also appeared, with conditions suitable for human life and cattle breeding.

I always remind the visitor of the following: when preparing for a trip to Patagonia, the traveler sees many pictures of lakes, forests, mountains, glaciers, and snow. And that's fine, but don't forget that what you see represents only 10% of Patagonia. The remaining 90% is this huge semi-desert, which for many seems boring, enigmatic and unfriendly. But it is in this region that the most important events in Patagonian history have taken place, and that is why we must give it the value it deserves.

We will see in the following chapters how this "boring" region became of interest to the South American governments, along with stories of the explorers and the impressions they gained from this region at the ends of the Earth.

Replica from the Nao Victoria in Patagonia. This ship completed the first trip around the world.
Photograph kindly shared by Luis Quezada.

CHAPTER 4

The strait of Magellan

After reviewing some 200 million years of the Earth's history, we can now move on to historical topics that are more tangible for us. It is not the same to talk about unimaginable times, such as millions of years ago, as it is to talk about what happened only 500 years ago. In this chapter is one of my favorite parts of modern history, and I hope you will find it enjoyable to read, especially as it will put Patagonia on the maps of the world.

These were times when explorations were made to the farthest corners of the world and numerous discoveries increased our knowledge of the cartography of the Earth.

This stretch of naval expansion added mysterious terrains that will attract the attention of the European society, with stories of these distant lands and maps that were named "*terra incognita*". Society will hear stories of "giants", or also of animals that were supposedly extinct, but which in these remote lands may still be alive.

After living in Patagonia for several years, I was able to understand that the idealization of a destination will always depend on how the story is presented and through whose eyes and pens these descriptions are written.

European context and Columbus' voyage:

From the middle of the 15th century Europe was seething with the search for new worlds, new ports, and new trade routes, largely due to the rise of the Turkish Empire, which put the crowns of Europe in turmoil. Spain and Portugal had divided the Atlantic Ocean in order to achieve a transitional peace.

The voyages of Christopher Columbus from 1492 onwards were aimed at finding a new route to the Indies, because with the theory of the roundness of the

Earth they wanted to avoid the foreign powers that lurked along the only known route around Africa, which was controlled by Portugal. When Columbus' company arrived in these new lands, they thought they had reached mainland Asia.

During these voyages in the area of present-day Panama, a sea of enormous size was sighted and named the "South Sea", which was not navigated because its passage had not been discovered. I mention this detail because it is a trigger for our story that has Ferdinand Magellan as the protagonist.

Columbus' discovery brought with it major friction with Portugal, as they had recently signed a treaty in which Spain and Portugal divided the Atlantic Ocean. Spain gave up its aspirations in South Africa and gained possession of the Canary Islands. The signed treaty did not take into account the real dimension of our world, hence the Portuguese reaction. Columbus claimed to have reached Asia via the Atlantic and Portugal claimed that, if the territories reached in that expedition were below the latitudes of the Canary Islands, these territories should be under Portuguese rule. Therefore, they wanted to avoid new disputes and, through the Pope, to reach a new agreement.

The Treaty of Tordesillas

Signed in that Spanish city, the Treaty of Tordesillas would mark the destinies of Spain and Portugal forever. Its purpose was to divide the dominion of the Atlantic Ocean between these two Iberian powers. Portugal's influence extends to about 370 leagues west of Cape Verde (actual Brazilian coastline), and beyond this line, Spain's influence begins.

This treaty was signed in 1497 after Columbus' voyage to America, although in those years they still thought it was Asia. The treaty was signed in this context, and thus determined the future of the Iberian crowns: Portugal was able to control the only known route at that time to the spice islands, the Moluccas, which today are part of Indonesia.

But why were these spices so valuable? The prestige of these products came from the lack of Europe's ability to keep food fresh, especially meat, which was sometimes consumed in a state that was not very pleasant to the palate. Hence the importance of spices such as cinnamon, cloves, pepper, nutmeg, ginger and many others. They were important for flavoring the product and making it more edible and appetizing, and also for medicinal use due to their antiseptic or digestive stimulant properties, to cite a few examples.

In the 15th century, in addition to the interest in obtaining spices directly and because of their increasing value, scientific advances (such as the compass and the astrolabe) and safer ships (caravels) enabled sailors to venture further and further afield. Portugal had reached the African coast and so secured a passage via the Cape of Good Hope to India and Southeast Asia.

Christopher Columbus died in Valladolid, Spain on 1506. He is considered the discoverer of America, although he died believing he had reached the Indies.

The new continent is named after another Italian explorer: Amerigo Vespucci, who took part in several expeditions to America in the early 16th century. In his diaries, Vespucci already wrote that these lands were not the Indies, but part of a new continent between Europe and Asia.

With this new information, the Treaty of Tordesillas (1494) seems to have become outdated, but without knowing it, both Spain and Portugal had already begun to influence the new World. Portugal had already established itself in what is now Brazil, which, according to measurements, was its territory. Spain would do the same with the other territories it had reached. In the long run, the area of influence of these powers would be tilted towards that of the Spanish crown. Although Portugal believed itself to be in a better position as it still had the only sea route to the island of spices: the Moluccas.

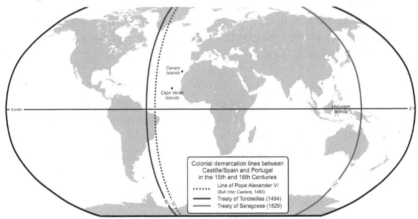

Spain_and_Portugal Lencer, CC BY-SA 3.0 via Wikimedia Commons

Portraits from "'Cristóbal Colón'" y "'Magallanes'" by Biblioteca Rector Machado y Nuñez under license CC PDM 1.0

Ferdinand Magellan

Magellan was born into a family of Portuguese nobility. He had a father who held important positions in the politics of the city of Porto. In his youth he was sent to Lisbon to work at the court of the Portuguese monarchy where he was able to receive a privileged education.

The news of Columbus and his "arrival in Asia" did not go unnoticed in Portugal, because Columbus had initially presented the project to the Portuguese crown but it was rejected and ended up being financed by Spain. This awakened in Ferdinand a spirit of adventure, thinking also that he would seek to help his kings not to surrender the supremacy of the Atlantic so easily. Magellan grew up in this environment, learned Latin and received a good education, but the wonders that were told of the Orient encouraged him to venture into the maritime and military sphere. At the age of 25, he enlisted in an expedition to India, where he began an important 8-year career where he gathered a lot of experience in Africa, Kerala, Cochin, and Goa. He took part in armed clashes for the control of the Indian Ocean, which he won. Some time later he took part in the attempt to settle in Melaka (Malaysia), the gateway to the Spice Islands, which was achieved in 1511 by Portugal. This consecrated Magellan as an important seafarer for his conquests. He returned to Lisbon to represent Portuguese interests in Morocco, where he suffered a leg injury that left him limp for life.

He returned to Lisbon, where he received a pension, although there were some accusations against him that tarnished his reputation, including cattle rustling and clandestine trade with the Moors, which was a forbidden activity. The negative effect of these accusations marginalized Magellan from leading new expeditions to the East, taking the spotlight away from a seafarer who was already accustomed to overseas adventures.

However, his long stay in the Lusitanian capital allowed him to hatch an idea, in which he wanted to visualize cartographically the real position of the Moluccas (Spice Islands). Lisbon had become the strategic place where the latest news on travel, cartographic and scientific development were concentrated. For these reasons, and adding his high qualifications and his contacts in the nobility, he was able to access exclusive material, such as the latest maps produced by prestigious cartographers like Martin of Bohemia, author of the first globe.

He began so to develop the idea of exploring another route to the Moluccas Islands via the Atlantic to the west, trying to find a passage through the south of the New World that would connect the East with Portugal through the recently discovered "South Sea".

Portugal says No, Spain says Yes

Magellan's idea was based on clarifying a very important doubt: he wanted to compare the compatibility of the Treaty of Tordesillas with the real position of the Moluccas Islands. The line drawn after Tordesillas went from pole to pole, and established the maritime limit of both kingdoms without contemplating the full extent of the globe. The "South Sea" had to be navigated to see if the Moluccas were really Portuguese or, perhaps, located under Spanish-influenced territories. Many cartographers theorized about their location, but for Magellan this did not solve the problem exactly. He had to study, prepare, and see this dilemma as a chance for a new overseas exploration. In 1516 he managed to meet with the Portuguese monarch Manuel I, taking the opportunity to deny the accusations against him. He then demanded greater recognition for his services and an increase in his pension, recalling the invalidity he brought back from his campaigns in Africa. The monarch did not accept his pleadings or his requests, and apparently did not go so far as to pitch this exploratory idea. The discredit and the stain on his personal prestige were already irreversible for the King. After that interview, Magellan was released to offer his services to other kingdoms.

At the same time that the Portuguese authorities were closing their doors to them, the direct competition of the Lusitanians in geographical discoveries quickly opened theirs. Spain had financed Christopher Columbus' expeditions, and now Magellan would present his project there.

Let us dwell for a second on Magellan's idea: would it be in Portugal's interest to finance an expedition that could confirm that the Moluccas rightfully belong to Spain and not to Portugal? Imagine just the disaster that this could have caused. Perhaps for this reason, Magellan kept the project for the Kingdom of Spain, where it would be viewed with greater interest.

Magellan moved to Andalusia, where he married a noblewoman and quickly became part of the upper echelons of the court. He gradually made contacts that brought him closer to the future monarch Charles I, who had a great interest in geography. He managed to present his idea using the brand new globes, astonishing the court. Then, with some conditions, they agreed to finance Magellan's enterprise. The news reached Lisbon and King Manuel I, having heard the news, tried to prevent Magellan from embarking on the expedition, which he failed to do. It is said that they tried to assassinate him and that the Spanish court put people under his protection.

Years later, in 1519, Magellan set out on behalf of the Spanish crown in search of a passage to the "South Sea" and with the aim of finding the way to the Moluccas Islands from the west to dominate the spice trade, since the known land route was in the hands of the Turkish empire.

Magellan's expedition: 1519-1522

In 1519, five ships and almost two hundred and fifty men set sail from Seville and, without knowing, they would change the geography of the world forever.

Crossing the Equator, Magellan sailed along the southern lands of South America, where he began to explore a territory that was already populated by civilizations, but which were then totally unknown to Europeans. For example, they passed through the Rio de la Plata believing it to be the passage to the South Sea, but only realized that it was a large freshwater river. Years later Buenos Aires would be founded at the mouth of this river.

In May 1520, the expedition arrived at a bay they named San Julián, on what is now Argentina's Atlantic coast. That stop provided the crew with their first encounter with the aboriginal population of that "new world": the Tehuelches.

The Europeans were surprised by their size and the enormous size of their feet; the footprints of those natives served as inspiration for Magellan to name this territory. He, like many people of the time who could read or write, was fond of novels. The theory is that the origin of the word could actually be in a Spanish book entitled "*Primaleón*": the main character was a giant called *Patagón*, who would have given him the idea of immortalizing the name of this territory as we know it today: Patagonia.

In the following months he found the passage between the oceans, which, although tortuous, he was grateful for; he named it the "*Paso de Todos los Santos*" (All Saints' Passage). It would later be known as the "Strait of Magellan". In this crossing process, which lasted about 3 weeks, one ship deserted and returned to Spain and the other sank. Many speculated that the deserting ship was following orders from Magellan, who would have acted as a Portuguese spy, although the ship would return to Seville and denounce that the leader of the expedition was committing abuses of power, which did not go down well in Spain.

Only three ships crossed into these new waters and, seeing how calm the sea was after the difficult crossing of the strait, this new ocean was inscribed on the maps as the Pacific. Nobody imagined how big this ocean was and it took them 100 days to find islands where they could resupply, affecting the morale of the crew, causing starvation and disease.

The first circumnavigation in history

Many mistakenly think that Magellan was the first to circumnavigate the globe, but in reality, Magellan led the voyage, but he died in the Philippine Islands. After reaching food-rich lands, he grew in confidence because he knew that the goal was near. Attempting to subdue the natives of Mactan Island, Magellan was killed in battle, where he was greatly outnumbered. Today a cross commemorates the sailor on these islands.

Other captains managed to reach the Moluccas, where they loaded the ships with precious spices, but one ship had to be burned for lack of crew and the other was left ashore to be repaired. Juan Sebastián Elcano showed extraordinary audacity, not only in taking command of the Victoria, but also in the way he approached his return to Spain. The fundamental objective was to reach Spain by sailing westwards, avoiding the Portuguese routes so as not to be detected and captured. For this reason, they made no stopovers and traveled away from the coast. If they succeeded, they would be the first to complete the round-the-world voyage.

The crew knew it was a suicidal mission and that they would be facing a previously unknown ocean in southern latitudes - the Indian Ocean. Then they had to pass the dreaded Cape of Good Hope, known to be a place where the currents and winds are always impossible to navigate, and then they had to sail up the Atlantic, always far from the coast. But the illusion not only of returning, but also of being the first to circumnavigate the world and to make history, would lead these men to reach their goal, although not without unforeseen events and, of course, without extreme suffering and the threat of almost certain death.

Eighteen men on the Victoria arrived in Seville three years later, with Elcano as captain.

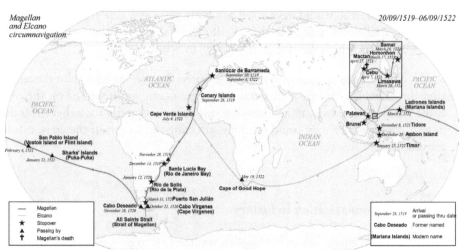

French map of the first world circumnavigation of Ferdinand de Magellan and Juan Sebastián Elcano, from 1519 to 1522.
Author: Sémhur and derivative work: Armando-Martin
CC BY-SA 3.0 - Wikimedia Commons

Summary of the Voyage

This voyage had three initial objectives and at least two of them were achieved. Firstly, a strait in the south of America had been discovered, providing the longed-for inter-oceanic passage. Secondly, the alternative route to the Spice Islands was found, avoiding the African route. Thirdly, it could not be proved that these islands were under Spanish jurisdiction, and in fact it was established that the archipelago belonged to the Portuguese crown.

Not negligible is the fact that the encounter of the Philippine Islands, which also offered similar riches, aroused hopes and would later end up in the Hispanic sphere of influence. Therefore, Spain and Portugal later signed the Treaty of Saragossa in which Spain recognized the Moluccas as a Portuguese dominion and Portugal ceded control of the Philippines to Spain.

But Magellan's voyage fulfilled a fourth, unforeseen objective: to sail around the world. Nobody thought of making such a voyage and there were two good reasons to avoid it: it was a voyage forbidden for Spanish-flagged ships in the Indian Ocean with the risk of capture and death at the hands of the Portuguese, added to the fact that it was a voyage that was highly unviable due to the lack of stops and, therefore, food. We remember that the enterprise was projected beyond Magellan and it was Juan Sebastian Elcano who took the glory.

Magellan's heritage in Patagonia

This trip changed the world, but it also served to put on the map this corner of the planet where, apparently, giants, or *patagones* as he decided to name them based on his readings, lived.

Magellan was a captain with some controversial decisions, but with a firm hand. He suffered mutinies and uprisings, as the expedition endured long periods of hunger, landlessness, cold, and uncertainty as to the success of the venture.

On reaching the coast of what is now Patagonia, he named the bay of San Julián, where he stayed for more than 150 days, spending the winter there. He then stationed a little further south at Puerto de Santa Cruz where, due to storms, he decided to wait for more than 50 days. Finding a pass, they turned west at Cape Virgenes, also named after this expedition. All these names have religious connections and it will be no different when they find the passage between the oceans, but as already mentioned, history corrected it to "Strait of Magellan". On this voyage, they documented that on the south coast from the ships, countless bonfires of the natives could be seen in what will be known as the Land of Fire (Tierra del Fuego).

Later, centuries later, many animal and plant species will also bear the name of Magellan in their taxonomy, thus giving the relationship that we are talking about this southern region of the planet. The magellanic forest, which refers to the Patagonian forest, and the magellanic penguin, to name but a few examples.

What did the discovery of the Strait of Magellan mean?

This discovery connecting two oceanic masses will be a turning point for navigation in the world. The Strait of Magellan puts Patagonia on the maps of the world.

I think Magellan did not expect the new Pacific Ocean to be so large, as it took him 100 days to find land and supplies were scarce, causing problems. The next sailors will take this into account.

Those images of sea monsters that were drawn on maps were demystified, and that everywhere they touched port they found cultures or civilizations of human beings, something that although it still seems silly, had to be confirmed. Seeing is believing.

For Spain and Portugal, it meant an escalation in tension between the two kingdoms, as Spain now had a new alternative route to the Moluccas Islands where the precious spices were to be found.

For the world, it sparked the emergence of a new connection between Europe and Southeast Asia that gave rise to trade and the transport of people between these two far-flung corners of the globe.

As I said, this is my favorite part of modern history, because we see that Magellan was perhaps a visionary. He used his intelligence to carry out an enterprise that was born out of using globes and not flat maps to understand what the world was like and to plan his expedition. It could be seen as the first step in a process that we know today as "globalization".

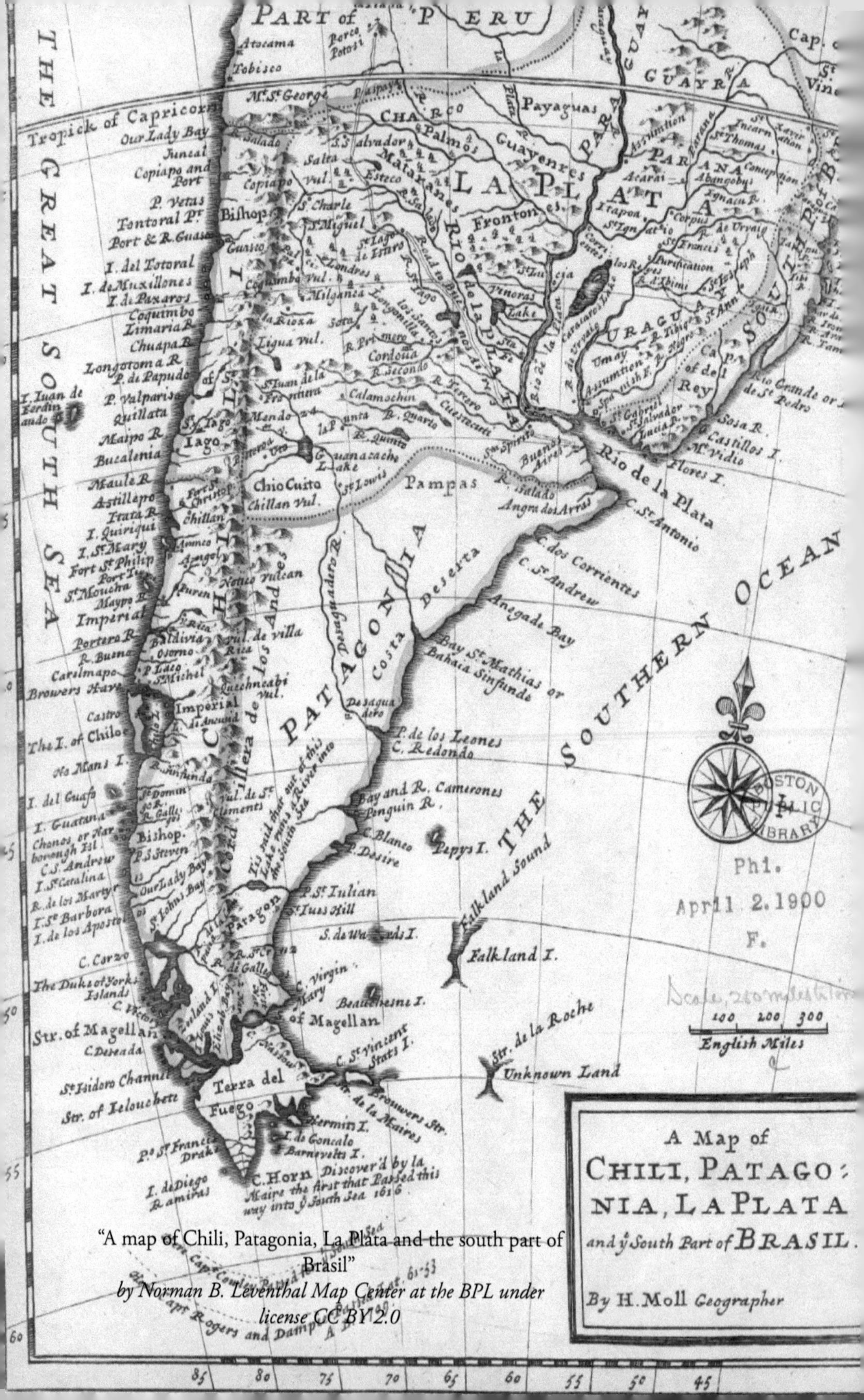

PART of PERU

THE GREAT SOUTH SEA

Tropick of Capricorn

CHACO

LA PLATA

GUAYRA

PARANA

URUGUAY

SOUTH B

RIO de la Plata

Rio de la Plata

PAMPAS

Buenos Aires

PATAGONIA

Costa Deserta

THE SOUTHERN OCEAN

CHILI

Cordillera de los Andes

Str. of Magellan

Terra del Fuego

C. Horn

Falkland I.

Falkland Sound

Str. de la Roche

Unknown Land

Pepys I.

Discover'd by la Mairs the first that passed this way into ye South Sea 1616

Scale, 260 miles to
100   200   300
English Miles

A Map of
CHILI, PATAGO-
NIA, LA PLATA
and ye South Part of BRASIL.

By H. Moll Geographer

CHAPTER 5

Late interest in Patagonia
1536-1880

The history of the territory where Argentina and a large part of Patagonia are located has been written over the last five centuries. I rewrote this chapter several times, because I wanted to find a story that would be easy to digest and, above all, understandable to the reader. For someone born in Argentina, it is easy to make a historical review of his country, since these are processes that one has known since school. But it seems to me that to go over this in a book about Patagonia can lead to confusion and open the doors to other subjects that have nothing to do with our area of interest. That is why I will do a rough overview on the historical processes that do not have Patagonia as their setting. That way the reader can understand the historical contexts for which it was not taken into account until the 19th century.

Something we already know from the previous chapter is that the Treaty of Tordesillas determined that almost the entire American continent would be under Spanish rule from the 15th century onwards, with the exception of present-day Brazil. After Magellan's expedition around South America, it was important for Spain to be able to settle in these territories. Spanish rule in the Americas lasted until the beginning of the 19th century, when the territories achieved a hard-earned independence and thus gave birth to the new South American nations.

Once again, I will make this historical journey as light as possible, separating two historical moments: the colonial era, and contemporary history.

The colonial period (1536-1810)

The colonial time took place when South America was under the influence of the Spanish crown. It all began in 1536, a few years after Magellan's voyage. An expedition on behalf of the Spanish crown under the command of Pedro de Mendoza

51

founded a rather primitive fort on the banks of the Río de la Plata under the name of *Santa María del Buen Ayre*. It was not easy for the crew, who starved and had to face the hostility of the natives of the Pampas. Some men returned to Spain, others sailed up the inland rivers to what is now Paraguay, founding Asunción. For many, this event, which took place in the Río de la Plata, signifies the first foundation of present-day Buenos Aires, although not the official one.

After a few years, from Asunción, the Spanish sent another expedition down the Río de la Plata. This expedition was made with the aim of not feeling cornered in Asunción and to ensure that they had an outlet to the sea. Then, this time under the command of Juan de Garay, and complying with the protocols of the time, the city of the Holy Trinity and the Port of Santa María de los Buenos Aires were definitively founded on 1580.

That way the Spanish began to gain strength in the territory, to stop the advance of the Portuguese who were already on the coast of present-day Brazil.

With the fundamental objective of defending Spanish positions in America, Spain began to establish new authorities in the New World in order to consolidate itself socially, economically and militarily, these authorities were called viceroyalties. The viceroyalty constituted the highest territorial and political-administrative expression that existed in Spanish America, and was intended to guarantee the dominion and authority of the Spanish monarchy over the newly discovered lands. It was the viceroy who represented the King's will in this territory.

The creation of the Viceroyalty of Peru, followed by the discovery of the Potosi mines, took place in the 16th century. This event is key, as it will finance the Spanish crown for the following centuries.

The difficulty lay in the distance, as this viceroyalty had no outlet to the Atlantic Ocean to send the precious goods to Spain. But here the role of Buenos Aires, which was just a village with an Atlantic port, began to gain momentum. Then it was decided that all the silver collected in the Viceroyalty of Peru could leave for Spain through the port of Buenos Aires on the Río de la Plata.

Buenos Aires began to take center stage, and the importance of this operation was vital for the Spanish crown, which decided to found the Viceroyalty of the Río de la Plata in 1776. The reasons for the creation of this viceroyalty arose from the need of the metropolis to defend this strategic position in the south of the continent from the ambitions of other colonial powers, such as England and Portugal. The territory demarcated by this Viceroyalty will become the base of the current territory of the Argentine Republic.

The economic monopoly between America and Spain was in force, and foreign powers wanted to trade with Buenos Aires, but the city was chained to trade only with Spain. These powers tried several times to invade Buenos Aires, but were repelled by the Spanish. That is to say that the interest and the eyes of Spain and the foreign powers were on Buenos Aires, the most active port in the region on the Río de la Plata, from where the riches obtained from the mines of Potosí in Peru departed for Europe. At this time there were too few human resources to take an interest in other territories, or to take part in battles that were not of great necessity, but rather to protect the interests of the crown in the acquisition of wealth. Patagonia up to this point had not developed much, apart from a few ports on the coast.

Revolution and Independence in Argentina (1810-1816)

A story perhaps more familiar to the reader is Napoleon's invasion of Spain, which ended with the capture of the King Ferdinand VII. This was a decisive event for the colonies in Latin America, as the King was no longer on his throne. Britain tried twice during these years of weakness, between 1806 and 1807, to take Buenos Aires, but the "*criollos*" (children of Spaniards born in America) were able to defend themselves. These victories over the English gave the criollos the confidence they needed to carry out a revolution in 1810 that would cut the chains with Spain, so that Buenos Aires could choose its own destiny. On May 25th, the criollos formed the first national government in what is known as the "*Revolución de Mayo*".

This revolution did not mean definitive independence, for the territory was large and the Spanish were still present in it, trying to vindicate the King's image. The criollos sowed a seed of independence that was defended with sabers and muskets, and Argentina only declared itself independent in 1816. The wars of independence that took place in these territories were always in the center, west and north of present-day Argentina. Patagonia had almost no Spanish military or revolutionary presence.

"La Revolución de Mayo" *portrayed by Francisco Fortuny (1910). Public Domain.*

The Young Argentine Republic (1816-1880)

Buenos Aires is historically the capital of the territory. This city had a 300-year head start over the rest of Argentina's provinces, as port revenues and investments over the years turned it into an advanced metropolis. The big problem was to agree on how this huge territory was now to be governed, and above all how the wealth was to be divided. This led to long years of civil wars, again concentrated in the center and north of the country.

Geographically, the national territory included La Pampa, Los Andes, La Puna, El Litoral and El Chaco. All this corresponds to the center and north of the country. The south (Patagonia) was to be treated with caution, because of the presence of the native peoples (of whom there was so much bad press). The south of South America was already known as Patagonia thanks to Magellan, but given the region's isolated location and harsh climate, it was postponed for annexation.

At the macroeconomic level, it was essential for the country to adapt to global changes, especially during the years of the industrial revolution. The world had been divided into industrialized countries and countries producing raw materials. This adaptation required Argentina to position itself as an exporter of raw materials to the most industrially advanced countries. To achieve this, the country had to put to work the large tracts of fertile pampa land, although Argentina could still offer much more room for growth.

Paint of President Julio Argentino Roca before the Congress (ca. 1886-1887)
by Juan Manuel Blanes - Buenos Aires Ciudad, Public Domain.

By the end of 1870, the Argentine government decided that it was imperative to take definitive possession of the southern territories in order to annex land for agriculture and livestock farming. The great challenge for both Argentina and Chile were to be able to populate these distant lands, as the scarce population of both countries was concentrated in and around the cities of Santiago and Buenos Aires. It was therefore imperative for these nations to be able to speed up the arrival of inhabitants who wanted to settle and work the land in Patagonia.

Also, the worrying border situation between Argentina and Chile over control of Patagonia and the Strait of Magellan put the ruling class of both nations on edge. If the reader can look at the map of Patagonia, he can see at a glance the reason: whoever could gain control of this territory could afford the luxury of having a nation with access to both oceans.

Also worrying was the presence of foreign powers, such as the British, French and Dutch, who increasingly frequented these southern waters, such as the Falkland Islands and the waters near Antarctica where whaling was a silent business that brought much wealth to the powers of the northern hemisphere.

Under pressure from regional factors, Argentina and Chile had to start defining and defending their positions and interests in regards to Patagonia.

International factors also demanded quick solutions, as the industrialized world's shortages looked favorably on South America and Australia. These two territories, with their vast tracts of land suitable for growing crops and livestock breeding, hoped to position themselves as major exporters of raw materials.

These territories will have to, at the very least, sort themselves out internally and cover their shortcomings in order to then build a project for a country that is aligned with this moment in world history.

How will Argentina establish itself as a leading producer country to supply markets in the northern hemisphere?

Francisco Pascasio Moreno and Emilio Frey in Patagonia.
Photo: *Archivo General de la Nación Argentina.*

CHAPTER 6

Patagonian and Fuegian explorations

By 1870, Patagonia was an urgent issue for both Argentina and Chile. And there was a great lack of information about this region. Although many ships would later begin to come to the South Seas, very few would come for truly exploratory or scientific purposes.

Here I am going to review some of the most interesting events that took place during the years in which the story is unfolding. As I said before, I want to try to make the book as chronological as possible so that it is easier to order the events that took place in this part of the world.

Just to clarify what the title says: Patagonian Explorations refers to explorations taking place in mainland Patagonia, i.e. from the Strait of Magellan northwards. When I refer to something "Fuegian" I mean the island of Tierra del Fuego and minor islands, i.e. from the Strait of Magellan southwards to Cape Horn.

(1834) Darwin in Patagonia: The Voyage of the Beagle

In 1834 the HMS Beagle sailed for the second time in Patagonia. This time as part of a round-the-world voyage for scientific and nautical purposes. She had previously made a first voyage for hydrographic purposes, and in April 1834, the Beagle returned to these lands with Darwin and Fitz Roy on board.

The Beagle stopped at the mouth of the Santa Cruz River, where they took the opportunity to carry out maintenance work. At that time, they decided to organize an expedition to go up the river, which carries turquoise water from the 'aciers of the Andes. Darwin and Fitz Roy (the captain) were very interested, a   uld not imagine where such a fast-flowing river with such characteristics · source. They prepared three whaleboats, provisions, and a team of

According to the chronicles, there were 25 men in total, enough to face the Indians, a matter that made them uneasy.

Going up the river was not easy. They suffered from the cold and at times the trip was very monotonous. They had provisions for three weeks, but the demands of the crossing were so intense that the discouraged Captain Fitz Roy, already short of provisions, decided to abandon the journey and return to the Beagle. Although it was cut short, that trip inaugurated a tradition of attempting to go up the Santa Cruz River, as we will see later on.

Darwin and Fitz Roy left several maps where they named various places on the river, such as Keel Point, Condor Cliff, and the "Mystery Plain": after the flat, barren place that forced them to turn back for lack of food to continue. Honestly, they were very close to the great lake that was the source of the river.

The Beagle traveled through the southern channel of Tierra del Fuego, the actual Beagle Channel as they've discovered it on the first voyage.

On that first voyage, the crew crossed paths with the *Yámanas*, who tried to rob them, and finally four of these natives were kidnapped. They were taken to England where they were taught the "arts of civilization", English and religion in the hope of being returned to their homeland so that they could preach what they had learned among their peers.

On this second voyage of the Beagle, they have the opportunity to return the abductees to their native Tierra del Fuego: unfortunately, only three returned, as one of the natives died on the voyage. Only two boys and one girl were returned, hoping that the plan would work: but it was a failure. Not long after being released, their clothes were torn and they went back to behaving as they had done all their lives until the abduction.

Darwin and Fitz Roy's journey around the world lasted approximately 5 years. After this trip, Charles Darwin would begin to elaborate the theory that catapulted him to fame. Darwin never traveled again. But in his mind, and according to his autobiography, the images of the immense Patagonian deserts and the forest-clad mountains of Tierra del Fuego had left an indelible impression on him. Patagonia stayed with Darwin until the end of his days.

Photograph of Charles Darwin; the frontispiece of Francis Darwin's The Life and Letters of Charles Darwin (1887) has the caption «From a Photograph (1854?) by Messrs. Maull. And Fox. Engraved for Harper's Magazine, October 1884.»

Darwin's notes on that trip up the Santa Cruz River extracted from his journal:

"*The country remained the same, and was extremely uninteresting. The complete similarity of the productions throughout Patagonia is one of its most striking characters. The level plains of arid shingle support the same stunted and dwarf plants; and in the valleys the same thorn-bearing bushes grow. Everywhere we see the same birds and insects. Even the very banks of the river and of the clear streamlets which entered it, were scarcely enlivened by a brighter tint of green. The curse of sterility is on the land, and the water flowing over a bed of pebbles partakes of the same curse. Hence the number of waterfowl is very scanty; for there is nothing to support life in the stream of this barren river.*"

Patagonia, a cursed land. Was he right?

(1877) An Argentinian expedition led by Francisco Pascasio Moreno

After the Beagle voyage, there were a few Argentine expeditions to the southern territories, although they had more practical objectives such as reconnaissance, mapping, and above all security for the small populations. But with pressure from the government to carry out acts of sovereignty in Patagonia, it was decided to sponsor Francisco Pascasio Moreno. He was a young man inspired by great naturalists with already a couple of trips to Patagonia with scientific motives, collecting fossils and making notes. He set out for the unknown land in 1876, with the aim of finding the source of the Santa Cruz River.

The young Moreno carried with him the notes Darwin had written 42 years earlier and paid attention to every reference of his journey up the Santa Cruz River.

In January 1877 they set out on the journey upriver. Moreno was on foot directing the maneuver, collecting objects for his collections, and comparing the route with Darwin's accounts and never ceasing to be amazed at the admirable precision of the maps.

They then camped in many of the places where the English naturalist had previously camped. After arriving at the "Mystery Plain " the rest was pure adventure. A week later they made a great discovery. Crossing a dune, Moreno spotted an enormous body of water that stretches to the foot of the Andes and the mission was accomplished: they had found an immense lake, which Moreno named forever "Lago Argentino".

Today, Lake Argentino is the largest lake in the country with an area of 1,500 square kilometers. Large glaciers discharge their turquoise-coloured water into the lake bed, which its colour is due to glacial sediments.

The naming of the lake was one of the many acts of sovereignty that Moreno carried out, as well as making detailed maps of it, in order to make it clear that this geography is no stranger to the Argentine government which, from Buenos Aires, had little influence in such distant territories.

DR. D. FRANCISCO P. MORENO
PERITO ARGENTINO EN LA DEMARCACIÓN DE LÍMITES CON CHILE

Francisco Pascasio Moreno by "La ilustración sudamericana" (1898)

Francisco Pascasio Moreno wrote a book about his journey, and some years later he gave lectures in Europe where he was awarded a prize by the *Royal Geographical Society*, London. There he gave the first photographic exhibition of Patagonia: a land of mythology of which only stories existed. Also, he presented his findings, and many people laid their eyes on a Mylodon skin, generating a lot of rumors in the scientific world. But that is another story.

(1901) Hesketh Prichard and the Mylodon

As said, Francisco Pascasio Moreno gave several dissertations at the *Royal Geographical Society*.

There he referred to a skin - which he took with him - found in a cave in southern Chile by the German settler Herrmann Eberhard. The skin was in excellent condition and was then studied and found to belong to a Mylodon. According to studies, these animals had been extinct for thousands of years.

The Director of the British Museum of Natural History said that it was "very likely" that the animal was still alive deep in the mountains of Patagonia. After hearing this, private individuals were organizing expeditions to find and hunt it. In those years, Cyril Arthur Pearson created the British newspaper *Daily Express* and, taking advantage of the great in-

Hesketh Prichard (1901) Credit: George Newnes Ltd. Public Domain

terest generated by the idea of finding a living Mylodon, he thought it appropriate to send an expedition to Patagonia and to publish regular articles in the brand-new paper, which sought to generate a large number of subscribers.

Hesketh Prichard, a young man eager for adventure, undertook the new quest. Many of his contemporaries thought he was a phony for deciding to set out in search of the Mylodon. But neither Pearson nor the journalist were naive. They probably knew that the search for the animal would be fruitless, but they could still capture the attention of readers.

Prichard landed at Puerto Santa Cruz, and with his companion marched on horseback inland along the banks of the Santa Cruz River. He also had Darwin's map, the one Moreno had used years before, confirming that this map was highly accurate for any traveler.

The journalist wanted to reach Lake Argentino and explore the North Arm, as Moreno indicated that there was a river coming from a large hidden lake. For this reason, more than finding the mylodon, the young journalist wanted to reach that river. With that objective in mind, in order to continue his march towards the mountain range, he needed a boat. Ernesto Cattle, an English inhabitant of the Lago Argentino area, helped him to recondition an old-little steam boat. They finally made it to the bottom of the North Arm, to the mouth of a sizable river that he named Caterina River, in memory of his mother. There they camped and continued upriver in search of the source of the Caterina River in the small canvas boat. Prichard continued alone anddiscovered a small lake. He named it "Pearson", in memory of his patron and financier. In that valley and after a year in Patagonia, he decided to put an end to his expedition.

Two years later, in New York, Prichard compiled the notes published in the Daily Express. He published a book in which he did not make a reliable record of the presence of the mylodon, but he did give an authentic account of the customs of the time. The book is called "Through the Heart of Patagonia"

(1908) The expedition of the Uppsala University professors

According to Carl Skottsberg's account, three Swedes from the University of Uppsala were in the Lago Argentino area: first they came from Antarctica and then they embarked on an adventure in Patagonia, described in a book called "Wilds of Patagonia".

There, Skottsberg shares the notes of Percy Quensel, who leaves the expedition to sail what he calls the South and North "fjords"(or arms of the Lake). Quensel would use the same boat as Prichard, as he retrieves it from the same person, Ernesto Cattle, who gives it to him; he travels the Canal de los Témpanos, taking two days to reach the Perito Moreno Glacier, formerly known as Bismarck, continuing south to the Frías Glacier.

He then continued the expedition north to cross the *Boca del Diablo* (Hellsgate – the narrowest part of the lake). He tried to go towards the area of the present Spegazzini Glacier, but the bad weather discouraged him and he decided to travel towards the northern glacier, where he found a large number of icebergs and, hidden behind a promontory (estimated to be the Herminita Peninsula), the largest glacier that Percy Quensel had seen in Patagonia.

He decided to call it Uppsala, after his university, while admiring the massive granite massifs that accompany the panorama. (Upsala in spanish)

Unfortunately, he had no more time, as he had to return to meet his friend Skottsberg and continue on to Chile.

Today the Upsala Glacier is one of the largest in the Argentine Republic, and has the particularity that its front is floating on the lake and it generates enormous icebergs that "decorate" Lake Argentino. This huge glacier is studied by Pedro Skvarka who used to be a climber and today is a renowned glaciologist who has a museum in El Calafate called "Glaciarium" dedicated to a life of work in the Patagonian Ice Field.

Percy Quensel, Carl Skottsberg y Albert Pagels in Patagonia, 1907.
Author unknown. Public Domain.

Summary

In this chapter we saw how cartographic and scientific knowledge of the patagonian region was slowly being obtained. This search for information was of great value to both governments at the time, who wanted to exercise immediate sovereignty over these precious territories.

At the time of Moreno (the character we mentioned before), Patagonia was only partially known through the writings of Darwin, who described it very negatively.

These trips served to provide more accurate and truthful information about Patagonia and what exists in these latitudes, not only for the governments of Chile and Argentina, but also for European societies. I regret not being able to include other summaries of expeditions, but the list is extensive and I have chosen the ones I know best and which have a certain relationship with each other.

The expedition of Moreno, in this respect, will be decisive later on in our book.

Upsala Glacier and its huge icebergs in 1960.
Photo: Archivo del Instituto Nacional del Hielo Continental Patagónico.

Presidents Julio A. Roca (Argentina) and Federico Errázuriz (Chile) on the Magellan Strait in 1899, signing a peace treaty.
Author: Spencer y Cia, Santiago - Valparaíso, Public domain, via Wikimedia Commons

CHAPTER 7

The border disputes between Chile and Argentina (1810-1902)

With Chile sharing more than three thousand kilometers of common border with Argentina, it is not surprising that border conflicts between the two nations have occurred so frequently. It is surprising that these conflicts have not turned into armed confrontations. Two young nations that were gradually advancing towards the far south of the planet realized the importance of the strategic situation of the region. At that time, the Patagonian region had an economic and productive potential that was ideal for the moment of instability in the northern hemisphere.

In this chapter I will describe the political moment that was taking place on both sides of the Andes and the urgencies that the countries had not only for Patagonia, but also for the rest of their territories.

The historical reference: *Uti Possidetis*

Due to the large territorial extension and the small population of the new republics, there were no problems in the first years of their existence regarding to their boundaries. In America, the principle of *Uti Possidetis* was applied, i.e. the fact of possession was accepted in the sense that the new states were left with the territories they had held in Spanish colonial times at the time of the revolutions in both countries in 1810.

Since the Conquest, the governments of Chile exercised jurisdiction beyond the Andes Mountains. The creation of the Viceroyalty of the Río de la Plata with its capital in Buenos Aires incorporated the territories at the centre, north and west until the Andes into the new jurisdiction, but the territories south of Buenos Aires were left under the authority of the Captaincy General of Chile.

The first border dispute for Argentina occurred in 1843 when the Chilean government founded Fort Bulnes on the Brunswick peninsula, on the shores of the Strait of Magellan. Fort Bulnes became today's "Punta Arenas" and was for many years the virtual capital of Patagonia due to the strong naval traffic in the area. The foundation of Fort Bulnes by Chile ignited the claims of Buenos Aires to dominion over the Strait of Magellan in December 1847. Buenos Aires, mired in a civil war, could do little in terms of warfare. In any case, this first disagreement gave rise to complicated diplomatic negotiations that lasted for more than thirty years.

Eventually, a conciliatory trend would begin in South America that would call on these young countries to settle their disputes diplomatically. It all began with the Spanish government's aggression against the countries of South America between 1864 and 1867; for example, the bombardment of Valparaíso (Chile) and Callao (Peru) in 1866. Then there was the establishment of the Empire of Maximilian of Habsburg in Mexico. All this was the fuel that could have stimulated this "Americanism" in many Latin American countries as a reaction to Spanish and French intervention.

In time, Argentina and Chile would sign a treaty of Peace and Friendship in order to settle these conflicts amicably. In any case, there were still wars in South America over boundaries, and this was often used to influence and exert pressure in the negotiations.

Initially they decided to turn to historians so that, according to the Cédulas Reales (Spanish cartographic documents), they could elucidate which territories really belonged to each country. But with so many incomplete and inaccurate versions, it was difficult to find a direction for the discussion.

The boundaries in force since 1810, discussed in the framework of diplomatic negotiations between Argentina and Chile between 1856 and 1881, were not clarified. There was no agreement between historians of the two countries. Each nation developed its own founding thesis: for the chileans, all of Patagonia belonged to Chile; for the argentines, southwards, all the territory belonged to Argentina.

The 1881 Treaty: Peace and Friendship

Until before the treaty, the borders of Latin American countries were established under the principle of *Uti Possidetis*. It is for this reason that the Republic of Chile possessed the whole of what is now southern Argentina, i.e. eastern Patagonia and the whole of Tierra del Fuego. However, with the treaty of 1881, Chile gave up a large part of its territory in order to achieve peace and friendship between the two countries.

This was because by 1881 Chile's international relations were not at their best: Chile had not yet been able to put an end to the armed conflict it had been involved in with Peru and Bolivia, known as the "Pacific War". On the other hand, the great powers, which had been harmed by the conflict, were unfriendly towards Chile and were prepared to put pressure on it in order to put an end to the situation in any way they could. Argentina, taking advantage of Chile's weak position, pressed for the signing of this "Treaty of Peace and Friendship" by purchasing state-of-the-art naval war machinery.

While Chilean forces were advancing north, Argentine forces were advancing south. The conflict broke out, and in the midst of a potential war, on 1881, Chile was almost forced to reach an agreement with Argentina and sign a boundary treaty.

This treaty fixed in general terms the geographical conditions of the future border demarcation, establishing that this would be the line dividing the waters of the two basins of the Andes Mountains.

Borders of Chile and Argentina

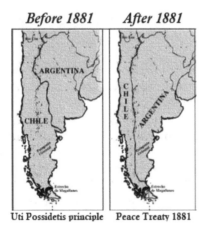

Before 1881   *After 1881*

Uti Possidetis principle   Peace Treaty 1881

In this way, Argentina ensured that Chile's advance to the east of the Cordillera would be prevented. However, this treaty meant for Chile giving up its historical rights over eastern Patagonia and this was very positive for the Argentine ruling class.

President Errázuriz visits President Roca boarding the battleship Belgrano (1899)
Source: Caras y Caretas n. 22, Public domain, via Wikimedia Commons

Chile secured sovereignty over the Strait of Magellan, one of the Chilean delegation's strategic interests. Further south, imaginary lines were used, as on the island of Tierra del Fuego, where a line arbitrarily divides the island in two, leaving the Atlantic and southeast coast for Argentina. The Pacific coast of Tierra del Fuego would belong to Chile, as would all the islands south of the Beagle Channel as far as Cape Horn and those to the west of Tierra del Fuego.

Finally, it was agreed in this treaty that, if any disputes were to arise in the future, this would be arbitrated by a third country, preferably a foreign power friendly to both nations.

In this way the problem was solved from a legal point of view, and later a symbolic event took place in the Strait of Magellan, where the Argentine and Chilean presidents met on ships from both countries. This meeting was called "the embrace of the Strait".

The experts and the 1902 arbitration

As mentioned in the previous paragraphs, the 1881 Treaty established that if there were difficulties in the demarcation of the boundary line, these would be resolved amicably by two experts representing each of the nations. If no agreement is reached, a third expert from a neutral country proposed by both governments will be called upon to decide.

Not long after signing this treaty the differences began again, especially in the valleys formed by the bifurcation of the Andes Mountains. There the watershed is not clear and the principles held by the two sides were irreconcilable.

The title of "*Perito*" is given to people who have extensive knowledge of a subject and who are experts on the matter. In this case, the Chilean and Argentinian experts, based on their knowledge of the region and geography, will defend their positions on the matter of the borders at the desks in Buenos Aires and Santiago, respectively.

The Chilean expert, Diego Barros Arana, upheld the principle of the continental watershed as the sole criterion for demarcation. This means that the border will be taken into account following the course of the rivers if they are of Atlantic or Pacific slope. And as explained above, in some Andean valleys, it is difficult to mark the division following this principle alone.

The Argentinean expert was a well-known figure, Francisco Pascasio Moreno (now Perito Moreno). With his experience of numerous trips to Patagonia, he based his theory on the continental watershed, but relating it to the high peaks. This made the demarcation clearer, but of course it was also in Argentina's interest to make this decision, as it would be able to defend disputed land in the mountainous area of northern Patagonia.

Moreno's knowledge of the Patagonian terrain gave him indisputable authority to tackle the serious conflict. No one was as knowledgeable and qualified to defend the Argentine position in this respect as he was. Everyone knew that Moreno had known those Andean solitudes, facing dangers and solving the labyrinths between mountains, valleys, rivers, and lakes with the aim of extirpating the mystery of the frontier.

In 1898 it was agreed to appoint Great Britain to settle as final arbiter the differences following the agreement between Argentina and Chile.

Sir Thomas Holdich was appointed by the British crown to visit the disputed areas. During this tour, Holdich was able to clear up his doubts and confirm his view of the Andean massif and the watercourses that flowed down both sides of the mountain range. He also noted that the Argentine maps were closer and more accurate than those provided by Chile.

In 1901 Perito Moreno accompanied the Commissioner of the Arbitral Tribunal, Thomas Holdich, on the reconnaissance from Patagonia. On this trip, they were to define the fate of 90,000 km2 of disputed mountain land.

The English arbitrator did not accept the continental watershed theory from Chile and while he favored Moreno's theory, he was also influenced in his decision by the populations of the territories they had visited on their voyage.

Boundary Commission of Argentina and Chile. Francisco Moreno, Clemente Onelli, Sir Thomas Holdich, and members of the Commission touring the region between Lake Lácar and the Última Esperanza sound, 1901.
Photo: Archivo General de la Nación Argentina. Inventario 51856.

In 1902 King Edward VII's decision was issued, and this was held in Argentina. It was 54,255 versus 39,915 square kilometers given to Chile and Argentina, respectively. The numbers seemed to favor one of the parties, but in reality, they were misleading figures, as they spoke more of quantity than of the quality of the soils in those territories, such as the valleys of northern Patagonia.

So, the Perito Francisco Pascasio Moreno became part of the great history of Patagonia, for his tireless work. His remains rest on Centinela Island in Bariloche, where passing ships sound their horns three times as a sign of respect for one of Patagonia's sentinels. Today he is remembered with a glacier that bears his name in the vicinity of Lake Argentino.

Left: Francisco Pascasio Moreno, no date.
Author: Malena Blanco. Archivo Museo "Juan B. Ambrossetti", Public domain, via Wikimedia Common
Right: vessels paying respects before isla Centinela in the Lake Nahuel Huapi – Bariloche area.
Source: argentina.gob.ar under license CC BY 4.0.

This seems to be the end of the border disputes, but tensions between the two countries will return in the future.

Historically, the problems between Argentina and Chile switched on or off according to the governments in power. At various times in the 20th century, people feared for a war. Socially, today there is an invisible rivalry between Argentina and Chile that does not go beyond jokes when it comes to political or football comparisons.

Back to our story, peace is now momentarily assured and the situation on the borders of Patagonia is calmer. This pacification, along with the promise of stability and security, was one of the keys to start bringing new settlers to Patagonia.

Potrait of Julio Argentino Roca, former
Argentine president who led a genocide
against the native peoples.
*Alexander S. Witcomb (1835-1905), Public
domain, via Wikimedia Commons*

CHAPTER 8

Argentina's southward expansion

In this chapter we will look at the first strategy applied by the Argentine government in order to implement the ambitious plan to add Patagonia to its national territory. With this target, the first step towards the sought-after "National Organization" would be taken, a historical process which began in 1880 and which today is the subject of study in Argentine schools.

This process of "National Organization" was driven by the Argentine ruling class, which was divided between the politicians who kept themselves in power through fraud. The fraud came from the votewhich was "sung", meaning, it was not secret. Whoever dared to challenge the ruling class had to face the consequences.

This process was also under pressure from big landowners and foreign powers who lobbied in the Argentine capital to take advantage of the vast territories in the south in order to exploit them.

To this end, one of the most studied presidents in Argentine history, President Julio Roca, laid out a military plan to wipe out the scattered but uninterrupted native peoples of Patagonia.

The modus operandi was to strip the pre-existing peoples of their sovereignty. Three operations were carried out: first, to construct a stereotype in which the indigenous people were considered a threat to the security of the nation by labeling them as barbarians. By talking about these "barbarians" it was established that their way of life had to disappear in order to assimilate into civilization. Their only possibility of integrating was to abandon their identity, their way of life and above all to abandon their lands.

Secondly, open violence was applied, which we will see later in the subtitle "the Conquest of the Desert". Many wanted this event to go down in history as a war. Now is beginning to be reviewed and catalogued as genocide: this violence includes concentration camps, mass deportations over hundreds of kilometers, torture and distribution of people against their will for forced labor, among other purposes.

Thirdly, it was followed by silencing: very little was said about it until a few years ago and the historical review of these episodes, like others that are also part of this book, deals with them in a very casual manner.

"The Conquest of the Desert"

This was the name given to the military campaign that began in Buenos Aires in 1779 and ended in Patagonia in 1885.

For a very long time, Buenos Aires was the southernmost city on the Atlantic coast of South America. South of Buenos Aires the region was considered "the desert", and remained occupied by its native inhabitants until this military operation.

With this campaign, the Argentine government wanted to completely dismantle the societies of native peoples, in this case the aforementioned Tehuelches; these nomadic Patagonians who lived by hunting the guanaco and choique. The aim was to disarm the groups living in the south of the country and eliminate their way of life in order to put a definitive end to this apparent threat, which the Buenos Aires authorities considered a hostile presence that made it difficult for them to integrate Patagonia into Argentina.

The Tehuelches had already undergone great changes brought by the settlement of ports, fortifications, farmers and stock breeders in the region. The incorporation of the horse had given them the possibility of traveling long distances, leaving behind the pedestrian phase that had accompanied them since the beginning of time. But the technological advances of the adversaries representing national political interests left the Tehuelches with almost no chance of even defending themselves on equal terms.

It is estimated that 6,000 soldiers participated in the campaigns that occupied Patagonia, in this genocide of the native peoples, which for many years in Argentina was treated as an issue from the European point of view, and without the opportunity to vindicate the native peoples.

Army on the Territory of Río Negro in 1879.
Photo: Antonio Pozzo - La fotografía en la Historia Argentina, tomo I, ISBN 950-782-643-2,
page 72
Public domain via Wikimedia Commons.

My approach here is not the same as that which the education system transmitted to me in my youth in Argentina. In the eyes of the new generations, this
was a genocide carried out by the ruling class in 1880, and not a simple military
campaign. It happened in Argentina, it happened in Australia, it happened in New
Zealand, it happened in many, many parts of the world in similar time frames. We
erased living history, just for economic and political interests. As a society, we must
take the blame then apologize and try to repair what was done.

In 1885, the last *cacique* (or chief) of the Tehuelches surrendered. Sayhueque
was the last of the great chiefs of the Tehuelche tribes in Patagonia, and he had no
choice but to surrender with his people after defending his lands and ideals with
great courage.

Unfortunately, when the Tehuelches were defeated in the Patagonian territory,
they were marginalized from the project to build the country: a large number of
Tehuelches died in this bloody and unequal battle, while many others were taken
prisoner and subjected to various forms of mistreatment ranging from slavery to
re-education.

The big sufferers were the native settlers, and the consequence of the defeat was the near disappearance of an indigenous people and culture.

Fortunately, today the Tehuelche culture is still alive and is gradually growing and opening up to the rest of the people who want to know, participate and spread this culture that was so persecuted in the past. It is possible to find books and many stories and legends that, thanks to their transcription, today will remain among the people who want to know and get closer to this millenary culture that inhabited the Patagonian soils since very distant times.

Tehuelches were apprehended during Campaña del Desierto.
Photo: "Mupiff. Indios prisioneros". From Carlos Encina and Edgardo Moreno, 1882-3, Archivo Museo Roca, Buenos Aires, Argentina. Public Domain.

The years after the genocide:

The national government after this "victory", celebrated by all the ruling class and landowners in Buenos Aires, set in motion its ambitious plan to populate these new lands annexed to the Argentine Republic.

With the defeat of the "adversary", the government set in motion its plan to divide Patagonia into different territories, each with a governor.

Finally, in 1884 the boundaries were marked and the new National Territories of Patagonia were organized, and from north to south these are: Rio Negro, Chubut, Santa Cruz and Tierra del Fuego.

Each of these new National Territories had a Governor, a Police Commissioner, and a Judge. Naturally, these were appointed arbitrarily from Buenos Aires.

By then, these large tracts of land were more uninhabited than before, as the campaign had drastically reduced the number of original inhabitants. There was now an urgent need to place Argentine or foreign settlers in order to make the occupation effective, trying to take advantage of the migratory phenomenon that was taking place worldwide, and also the economic moment with this International Division of Labor, where the southern hemisphere would be relegated to being a producer of raw materials.

Much land was given to friends of the ruling class as reward for their services. This provided for the donation of large portions of land to politicians and military personnel who had performed "outstandingly well" in the above-mentioned military campaign. In this way, it was justified to give away land in a disproportionate manner.

Another law sought to encourage immigration, granting land to those who required it, with the obligation to build housing and invest in order to produce with the land obtained. This type of law will be reformulated in each National Territory according to the conditions of the land and the needs of the place.

The migratory phenomenon, in any case, will provide Argentina with the amount of workforce needed to provide the necessary energy to the fields that will begin to produce raw materials, and will give the country that push that will position it in the place sought by the ruling class: to be one of the largest producers of raw materials in the world.

Now begins a chapter in Patagonian history in which we will see two types of people: the honest immigrants who came to Argentina to make a living, and the opportunists who sought to accumulate as much land as possible in order to amass disproportionate fortunes.

In the next two chapters I will detail the migratory phenomenon that took place in Argentina and then, how the new settlers organized themselves in the new Patagonian lands.

Kau: Tehuelche tents of guanaco skins. *Source: Archivo General de la Nacion, Inv. 316206.*

Two Tehuelche men at Tres Lagunas between Gallegos and Santa Cruz Rivers. *Source: Public Domain.*

Mess hall at "Hotel de los Inmigrantes" in Buenos Aires, 1910.
Source: Archivo General de la Nación Argentina, Caja 3241, Inventario 145103

CHAPTER 9

The great wave of immigration in Argentina (1875-1914)

To understand the important context of this moment in history, it is necessary to understand what happened to Argentina in the late 19th and early 20th centuries.

The world in 1880 was undergoing enormous changes through a historical process that empowered the countries of the Northern hemisphere: the Industrial Revolution. These nations were at a time of great technological developments at the industrial level that increased the production of manufactured goods to exponential levels, which generated in these countries a large demand for raw materials for alteration and commercialization.

A paradigm arises in the world with the international division of labor, where the fully industrialized northern hemisphere needed the supply of raw materials from the non-industrialized countries. At first, these countries began to source their supplies from their colonies, but this was definitely not enough: they needed new suppliers, countries with the ambition for development and with the potential territory to achieve these goals.

That is why in this chapter we will deal with one of the main phenomena of the history of the last century in the Western world: the great migratory movement towards America, and especially Argentina.

The local context:

As mentioned above, it was the ruling classes in both Argentina and Chile that relied on immigration as the phenomenon that could set both nations on the road to economic progress.

This path, marked by the encouragement of immigration, sought to populate the vast territories and provide the countryside with the necessary workforce to maximize production so that the countries could position themselves in the world as main exporters of raw materials.

Argentina had the ideal conditions to participate in this new paradigm and, at the same time, it had a strategic position on the world map that placed it in the middle of the commercial circuit between Asia and Europe through the Strait of Magellan. It was a golden opportunity, one that Argentina was able to seize.

By 1870, the concept of immigration as a factor of progress had been incorporated into national ideas. It was thought that the values of the European world would arrive along with a skilled workforce. This was thought in theory, but in practice it did not happen.

What was also intended was that these individuals would then become citizens through a vast universal education system. This was a slow process, but we can say that it was achieved in the end.

The idea of encouraging immigration had begun decades earlier, but it would not have positive effects until 1880-1910, when the peak of arrivals was seen. At the same time, it can be observed in this period of time that population census data show that people born in another country make up 30% of the country's total population.

Immigrants began to arrive for different reasons that varied according to their country of origin: lack of opportunities, poverty, hunger, political and social instability. In this sense, their experiences were the trigger for them to imagine living in such a remote and unknown place as Argentina at the end of the 19th century.

Argentina began to receive mostly Italians and Spaniards, followed by English and Scandinavians, and to a lesser extent Eastern Europeans and Middle Easterners. This mix, coupled with census data showing that immigrants made up a third of the national population by 1900, meant that Argentina, after the United States, was the second American country to receive immigrants.

The flow of Italian and Spanish immigrants will be constant until the middle of the 20th century, bringing with them a great influence that will modify customs and language. In short, Argentina has much to thank the immigrants who helped shape the national spirit.

Migratory influence

Knowing this, a tourist can see this in the architecture of the city of Buenos Aires, which presents colonial, Italianate, French academicism architecture and small details from other countries of the world.

The neighborhood of La Boca, in the port area, is a tribute to the immigrants who arrived and lived in these areas looking for a future. In the brothels of the port, men from different nations created a harmonic melody was born in these turbulent places: *the Tango.*

The reader may imagine the Tango as one of the dances of high society, but no. The Tango was born in the shadiest places of the time where the rootless gathered to seek solace to the rhythm of a melancholic music. Later it would be accepted by the upper class and then it would triumph in Europe.

The language spoken in Spain was imported into Latin America that came under its dominion, although over the centuries it was modified with regionalisms and then with the arrival of immigrants it underwent a complex modification. Especially with the appearance of a dialect known as *lunfardo*: a romantic mixture of Italian, Spanish and puns created to stay outside the law. An example of lunfardo is to turn words around so that the police could not understand.

The lack of housing meant that immigrants found accommodation in *conventillos.* Conventillos are boarding houses in the suburbs of Buenos Aires in which the immigrant population was housed. They consisted of many rooms around a central courtyard. Bathrooms and common areas like the kitchen were shared.

In Buenos Aires, the conventillos were located in the old part of the city, in the port of La Boca, where the jobs and opportunities were. The idea of the immigrants was to live there temporarily, but often they would stay there for decades. In general, the managers did not have a good relationship with the tenants and the hygienic conditions were poor. There was no privacy, let alone heating. Buenos Aires is very humid and cold in the winter and in the summers, it can get stiflingly hot. In daily contact they exchanged words, customs, meals, parties, prejudices, hopes and frustrations.

It is in these conventillos is where the cultures of different countries amalgamated, crossing lives that in any other circumstances would never have crossed.

Immigrants arriving to Buenos Aires, no date.
Source: Archivo General de la Nación - AR-AGN-AGAS01-DDF-rg- Caja 3241- Inventario 224356

Why was immigration important to Argentina?

For me, immigration in Argentina is a central topic because it gave the country that final blow, that turn of the screw, to finally become the country it is today.

Immigration to Patagonia was a little more complex, because it required labor, but also immigrants willing to adapt to the precarious living conditions offered in these lands. Patagonia is neither the Pampas nor Buenos Aires, and even today, the vast differences between these two regions of the country are noticeable. At that time, it was notorious that the eye of Buenos Aires did not reach this territory and could not see the shortcomings, but only the benefits offered by owning such large tracts of land to produce. For many years the mail and telegraph service were defective. The lack of authorities gave rise to corruption, generating discontent among small families who wanted to earn a decent living. Years later, this inequality would be translated into an uprising of the rural workers and would spark the famous Patagonian strikes.

The first to settle in Patagonia were the English immigrants who, appropriately enough, had already been settled for years in the Falklands and had become accustomed to the terrain, raising sheep that will easily adapt to the region. Clearly, Britain had realized the strategic and commercial importance of this area of the planet, where the most widely used inter-oceanic passage was located plus the potential capacity in this region to produce raw materials in large volumes.

In my research on the subject, I came to the conclusion that in Patagonia, generally immigrants coming from places with similar climates, such as Great Britain, Scandinavia, Central Europe and the Balkans, have become accustomed to the climate.

Many single immigrants came to Argentina, sent by their families with their life savings with the idea of being able to bring the other members of their families with them at a later stage. It has become clear over time that there are very few of these stories of reunions. This kind of uprooted life contributed to the melancholic and nostalgic spirit of Argentines.

Another type of immigration were the colonies: groups of immigrants from certain parts of Europe who came together to populate the country. There were many: French, Swiss, German and Italian colonies. These cases were immigration organized by the national state.

The story of the Welsh colony stands out in Patagonia. Here they found refuge while looking for a future to carry on their culture and religion in the face of persecution by the English crown. They suffered, like everyone else, the inclemency of the weather, the aridity of the soil, the difficulties of coexisting with the natives and, consequently, the economic problems of the expenses involved in adapting to this new life in this undeveloped region that is Patagonia. Today these stories bear witness to the histories of Puerto Madryn, Trelew, Gaiman and Trevelin which, among other towns, carry the Welsh heritage-

Regardless of the type of immigration, the state had the task of encouraging and protecting it.

The law encouraging immigration implemented various mechanisms to install special offices or consulates overseas. There were also free or discounted tickets. The big competition was the United States, where the journey from Europe was much shorter, and therefore much cheaper.

In Buenos Aires there was the *Hotel de Inmigrantes* (Pretty much like Ellis Island in New York), where the newcomer had free accommodation for the first few days and then free passage to his final destination in the country

What they wanted to do in this way was to favor rural colonization, and instruments were devised to facilitate the formation of colonies, although later on we will learn about some of the obstacles that prevented the migration plan from working as the government had intended.

Summary:

Between 1875 and 1914, Argentina received more than 5,000,000 people, representing 14% of the world's migratory movement at that time. It was thus the second country to receive immigrants after the United States.

9 out of 10 immigrants settled in the area of La Pampa, i.e. the center and east of the country, leaving a very small amount of people who settled in the most marginal regions of Argentina, such as Patagonia.

That is to say, the stories of immigrants in Patagonia were told by two types of individuals: the type who knew where they were going, people who had contacts of some kind that gave them the confidence to actually make the effort to live in lands as distant as they were inhospitable. Or the protagonists could be the type of people who arrived out of necessity, ignorance, chance, or deception.

And the most important is to understand the context in which this migratory process took place.

The northern hemisphere lived a duality between the progress of the Industrial Revolution and the political and social instability of the time. This opened the door for those without opportunities to go abroad in search of a better future.

After the independence of the region, the southern hemisphere needed settlers in order to put the general idea of progress on track. This idea of progress was based on an agro-export economy, driven by the new immigrant workforce and the vast tracts of land waiting to be worked.

It is impossible for me to enumerate all the changes that took place in Argentina during this great migratory process, because nothing remained unchanged. Urban and rural landscapes, language, customs and manners changed. Some things changed for the better and others for the worse. But, in short, it is impossible to talk about Argentina today without taking into account that formidable process.

Port of Buenos Aires, 1912.
Source: Archivo General de la Nación DDF Inventario 146213

Estancia Anita. Santa Cruz, Patagonia Argentina.
Photograph kindly shared by Juan Pablo Raposo.

CHAPTER 10

The phenomenon of the Patagonian Estancias

In this chapter, we will learn about the outcome of the end of the long process that began with the objectives of the Argentine ruling class. Occupation at any cost was achieved through the bloody slaughter of the native peoples in the infamous "Conquest of the Desert" and also through the resolution of the border problems with Chile, which left everything ready to begin the next phase. The great wave of immigration brought people from all corners of the world to populate Argentina, and very few ventured to Patagonia. The remoteness from urban centers and the harsh climatic conditions were not much favored by the newcomers. Many were misled by promises that were too good to be true. For example, with the promise that gold could be found in Patagonia, many arrived and found this to be a lie. Once in such a distant land, in order to pay their passage back to Buenos Aires, they had to work.

Patagonia was divided into *National Territories*, something like an autonomous provinces, but where the authorities were arbitrarily elected from the capital of the country.

Each governor was responsible for the installation of settlers to begin working the lands of each Territory, enforcing the immigration and settlement laws which in each one could differ according to need and urgency. The most common legal tool to achieve this was the lease.

How leases worked:

Each National Territory granted leases to those who came to settle Patagonia, regardless of where they came from. For what mattered was to settle in order to help the cause of the Argentine sovereignty, and also to produce raw materials for the country.

Immigrants arriving in Patagonia could request land from the governorates. Each governorate gave a predetermined number of hectares per family. For example, in the Territory of Santa Cruz, it had been agreed to give 20,000 hectares (50,000 acres) per family or tenant. Many will be surprised by the size of the parcels to be delivered, but let me tell you that a 20,000 hectare parcel can be considered small in vast Patagonia (I would sarcastically call it a "backyard").

When the request was accepted by the Territory's governorate, leases were signed between the interested parties. The conditions of the contracts changed over time and the demand for land in the region. One of the conditions was to produce wool, as the international market had a high demand for this product, which generated a high market value. A common example: 20,000 hectares were leased for 30 years. During those 30 years, the lessee had to pay annual taxes based on the usufruct of the land, and after 30 years, the lessee could access private ownership of the land. Often the access was 50 per cent and the other 50 per cent had to be bought from the government. But as I said, this is just to give examples.

It seems to be a very attractive deal. But let me tell you that living, or rather, surviving in Patagonia, is not an easy task, let alone a pleasure trip.

Origin of migrants:

As mentioned in the chapter on this subject, the national government's invitation to settle Patagonia coincided with a historical moment when part of humanity was moving from the Europe to America. They sought to make up for shortages such as food and freedom, in the hope of a better life.

Most of the immigrants were English. Many came from the Falklands Islands (*Malvinas*), where the English had been settled since 1833 in order to have a port to support their voyages to the Pacific Ocean through the Strait of Magellan. In the Falklands they had installed sheep that were able to adapt to the climate and which they would later import to mainland Argentina, precisely to Patagonia.

Australians, Scots, Yugoslavs, Croats, Scandinavians and Central Europeans, such as Germans, Swiss, Austrians, also arrived. Many of these immigrants lived in a new land, and now more uninhabited than before, these newcomers had to learn to build in solitude. Receiving a 20,000-hectare piece of land meant shutting themselves behind barbed wire fences in a field about the size of the city of Buenos Aires.

This first entry of English to the Patagonian coasts hinted at a trend that would mark the whole process of Patagonian occupation. These newcomers were already hardened by the wind and cold in their countries of origin; now they just had to get used to the solitude.

In Patagonia, the first settlers will be referred to as the "pioneers". Many of their stories coincide with the initial suffering. A search for new horizons in defiance of the hostile nature of these southern lands. But often these stories end with satisfied pioneers and their descendants. Other stories end in a dark and sad way. In this book I will try to present these two types of pioneers. I make this clarification, because from now on I will use the term "pioneers" to refer to these adventurous newcomers.

The Patagonian Estancia:

Estancia is the name given to the ranch, field, hacienda, where some kind of livestock was produced. The Patagonian Estancia is characterized by sheep production, i.e. sheep farming. The occupation of Patagonia took place at a time marked by the high international value of wool, when this raw material was required in enormous quantities. And so, the pioneers who settled on a 20,000-hectare plot of land founded an Estancia.

The foundation of the Estancia began with the fencing of the land, a well-paid task in the southern lands. Then they had to bring in the animals to start production. And finally, they had to build the buildings necessary for housing and the day-to-day running of a ranch. This group of buildings is called the *casco* (main buildings or main shed).

The main shed of an Estancia is the only place in 200 square kilometers where vital and necessary activities such as eating, sleeping and working take place. Normally this part of the Estancia must be protected from the strong and constant gusts of wind that sweep across Patagonia. This protection is normally done with tall trees, which must be planted and watered by each family. Remember that the Patagonian steppe is a semi-arid desert where the amount of rainfall is so minimal that it only allows shrubs to grow. In Patagonia is normal to find poplars and pines surrounding the buildings. These tall specimens act as a natural barrier that cuts the wind, which usually comes from the west.

It is also common to find small huts, distributed within the huge field. These are called *puestos* (outposts). In these outposts, the farm workers live for several months in solitude, looking after the animals while they graze at different times of the year.

In short, we have a large field, which we call Estancia because of its livestock-producing capacity. We have a group of main buildings which we call the main shed. And finally, the small posts where those who take care of the animals during the grazing seasons live.

Shearing shed of Estancia Anita. Note the poplars rising behind it.
Photograph kindly shared by Juan Pablo Raposo.

The architecture of the Estancias:

As I mentioned earlier, most of the immigrants were English. The architectural tendency then will be imposed by this British building trend which was based on elements brought from the industrialized world. Let us remember that 90% of Patagonia is steppe, and as settlement started from the coast to the west where the forests are, the available resources were not suitable for construction. The pioneering architecture consisted of two imported elements: corrugated zinc sheets and wooden planks.

The zinc sheets were shipped by boat where, due to their corrugated finish, they traveled stacked one on top of the other, taking up little space in the hold, but increasing the load capacity of the sheets. These zinc sheets were used as the outer covering of construction, not only for dwellings, but also for rural buildings such as shearing sheds, staff dormitories, kitchens and so on. Walls and roofs were covered with these sheets, providing a good protection that is still in good condition today.

At first the wood came from England due to the lack of resources on the Patagonian coast. But then it began to be brought from Punta Arenas, where *lenga*, a native Patagonian tree of the *Nothofagus* family, was traded. This wood has excellent properties for construction, as it can grow up to 30 meters high and its wood is semi-hard and very usable.

The skeletons of the American-style buildings, known as Balloon-Frame, were made from wood in a post-and-beam system. The skeleton was covered on both sides with more rustic wooden boards. The outside was then covered with corrugated zinc sheeting and the inside with newspaper. With this construction system, an air chamber was created between the boards, which was often filled with an insulating material such as sheep's wool, depending on the creativity of the builders.

This was the most common way of construction among the humble settlers of Patagonia and today they are a postcard of the southern region. Many times, tourists travel to Patagonia today to see the natural wonders and as a "bonus" take a tour to an Estancia where they are fed Patagonian lamb. Perhaps they fail to understand that the aim of the tour should not only be to eat, but to understand the historical importance that these buildings had for the region.

Mess hall and dormitories at Estancia Anita. We see poplars around it as well.
Photography kindly shared by Juan Pablo Raposo.

Other types of construction:

Many ranchers thought of greater comfort, and had the luxury of having prefabricated houses brought from England. There were catalogs where they could choose the format and number of rooms. These houses were built in England with the same materials and pre-assembled in their place of origin. They were then disassembled, numbered and shipped by boat to Patagonia.

I worked at Estancia Harberton in Tierra del Fuego, where you will find a prefabricated house and you could see how the house was still standing more than 100 years after it was built.

These types of prefabricated houses were of great help for rural settlements in isolated areas such as Patagonia and other islands in the South Seas. Also, many churches were built using these prefabricated kits.

As I mentioned, the influence of these English models left a mark on this region. Not only were their aesthetics adapted, but also the construction system and materials were really well adapted to the needs of the Patagonian region.

The appearing of large Estancias:

Normally a land petitioner would get 20,000 hectares of land. But there are always exceptions to the rule. For example, in those years, a sheep ranch of 200,000 hectares was approved by one of the governors of Santa Cruz. It is said that it was approved because 10 petitioners presented themselves in partnership, and thus one of the oldest and most famous estancias in Patagonia was created: *Estancia El Cóndor* in the Río Gallegos area. This is one of the many exceptions, as governors had attributes that allowed them to approve such agreements.

The national government was quite generous in the allocation of land in Patagonia and Tierra del Fuego. It gave a lot of land to foreign companies that would redistribute the land among immigrants, and also approved exaggerated requests for land to people who knew how to lobby in the offices and bureaus of the Argentine capital. With these exceptions to the rule, approved by an ambitious government that remained in power for many years by fraud, the first large Estancias were born in Patagonia.

These large Estancias took advantage of the historical moment of the high value of wool and brought in livestock technology from Europe, and also recruited the senior staff from these distant lands. These large Estancias became veritable sheep empires and were often a major problem for small ranchers. Many adventurers and globetrotters who came to try their luck in the region were soon evicted if the land they chose proved to be appetizing for the aforementioned big landowners.

Sight of an estancia in the middle of the immense Patagonia.
Photography kindly shared by Juan Pablo Raposo.

Summary:

The Estancias are a testimony to the Patagonian occupation. They are characterized by having been entirely dedicated to the production of wool due to the high value it had in these years on the international market. They are also characterized by being rooted in a large space, surrounded by an inhospitable climate and a lurking solitude.

The Estancia created a closed way of life, and was forged by the foreigner's adaptation to a cold, bitter and windy environment. Sometimes so windy that it even feels like the wind is trying to blow you away. First you had to arrive, and then prevail. Walking in this geography was by no means an easy task, and each Estancia is the symbol of a struggle won against an environment that resists any traveler.

Today we can say that the Estancias represent the foundational phenomenon of a sheep-breeding Patagonia, each Estancia being a population unit that was the genesis of the installation of the white man in these lands. If you take a detailed map of Patagonia today, you will see on the map not only the cities, of which there are very few, but also the Estancias that still occupy large areas in southern Argentina.

What's next:

Reading between the lines, we have seen how the government-sponsored settlement of Patagonia had some shades of gray, where the law was not equal for all.

The biggest mistake was to try to manage everything from Buenos Aires, from where it is impossible to control a vast territory so far from the eye of the law. They forgot that the new settlers needed clear regulations and effective controls: remember that the authorities were one governor, one police commissioner, and one judge designated from the capital of Argentina. This situation where there was a lack of authority and control generated situations of abuse, committed in pursuit of the greed and ambition of some in better positions such as the big landowners, who would greatly influence official decisions.

In any case, this absence of the state also motivated individual settlers to do their best to push forward the development of the region thanks to the strength and ingenuity they needed in the face of a lack of answers and resources. They had to solve these things on their own and without waiting for help, generating a self-sufficient society that opened roads, built bridges, irrigation canals, and generated a minimum infrastructure that both they and those who came later knew how to take advantage of.

The approximate route from the Great Sheep Drive in Patagonia. Map kindly shared by Sergio Zagier, Editorial Zagier & Urruty from the book "El Gran Arreo"

EL GRAN AF
Set. 1988/Jun.

ARGEN

© 2006 ZAGIER & URRUTY

250 km

CHAPTER 11

The great Patagonian sheep drive
1888-1890

In this chapter we are going to revisit one of the great almost forgotten historical events of the Patagonian region. A feat that today lives on thanks to the oral reproduction of the stories of those pioneers who sought to start dreaming big in the extreme south of South America.

A few chapters ago, we made it clear that one of the main external factors that boosted Patagonia's economy was the high demand for wool from the great European countries, and especially from the United Kingdom.

For many it is almost taken for granted that because Argentina is such a large country, sheep were already here and would multiply in a few years to meet the world's demand for wool. Even more so now that the immigrants are occupying the land little by little creating new productive units known as "Estancias". And as if two plus two equals four, we think that thanks to the sum of these factors, Patagonia became a sheep region. But it was not that easy.

To begin with, sheep are not native to South America, but were introduced by Europeans at the time of the conquest. Sheep production is still an important part of the Argentina's agricultural system. Traditionally, Argentina oriented sheep farming towards wool production, mainly in Patagonia, where the environment makes it difficult to develop any other agricultural activity.

Where do sheep come from?

It is estimated that the first sheep arrived to actual Buenos Aires around 1549. Some historians maintain that the first animals to arrive in the New World were Merinos, although it is also said that the first sheep were of the Syrian and Pyrenean breeds. This seems more likely, as Spain had then banned the export of the Merino breed.

The first large Estancias had been established in the Pampa region, around the port of Buenos Aires, where both cattle and sheep were worked, and these first estancias were to be the sources from which the Patagonian Estancias would obtain the livestock necessary to begin wool production.

Another, and perhaps more important, source of sheep for Patagonia was the *Islas Malvinas* or Falklands Islands, from where the animals came by ship to populate the vastness of the Patagonian steppe, and also the large island of Tierra del Fuego. The Falkland Islands are about 600 km away from Río Gallegos in mainland Patagonia, and only were populated by the British in the 1830s and had sheep farms, where the animals adapted very well from the beginning.

The first ranchers received the sheep from *Malvinas*, by ship, and arrived at different Patagonian ports such as Puerto Deseado, Puerto Santa Cruz on the Patagonian Atlantic coast, and the port of Punta Arenas, Chile, in the Strait of Magellan.

Ships could not carry large numbers of animals, so costs and results were not the best. We must also bear in mind that boat travel in the South Atlantic waters was very stressful for these animals.

The journey was so tortuous that it caused the animals great trauma, leaving them without the possibility of having offspring for one or even two full years. Also, the wool did not grow normally in the first year. Naturally this was to be expected, but for the ranchers it was a hard blow, as they always wanted to increase the number of animals in order to be able to produce more and more wool as quickly as possible.

That is why they gradually began to bring sheep from the center of the country, not by boat but by land. This made the process more natural for the animals, as they would always move on dry land, grazing as they went along until they reached their destination without having to spend a few weeks on the boats that ply the waters of the southern seas.

But we must pay some attention to this adventure. When we talk about "the center of the country", and we say that the destination is "Patagonia", we mean a distance of between 2,000 and 3,000 kilometers. That's to start with.

We must add to this distance, that we are in a windy, arid region, with little fresh water available on the way. In the winter, with very short days, the cold of the sea chills your bones and the winter snow make the marching very slow. And in the summer, with extra-long days, will not allow anyone to catch a break, as the work goes on longer than usual. The sunshine in summer is so strong that dries the land, and when the wind blows, it raises lots of dust blinding anyone.

In addition to the distance and the climate, there are the dangers that such a large-scale enterprise entails: for a group of men of European descent, the greatest fear at that time was to cross paths with warlike groups of Indians who would try to kill them or steal their animals. Another issue is the danger posed to the animals by the crossing of cold and rushing rivers, as well as the stalking of pumas or "mountain lions" who see the sheep as easy prey. Foxes can also be a problem.

And at last, sleeping in the open for as long as it takes to move the animals that far, the long hours of work in the Patagonian weather conditions, the monotony of the food and so on, will be the condiments of the most impressive and least documented adventure in Patagonia: The Great Patagonian Sheep Drive *(El Gran Arreo)*.

This was the name given to this enterprise which was conceived by pioneers who joined forces to transport approximately 5,000 sheep and almost 500 horses from the south of the Rio Negro to the south of the Territory of Santa Cruz in continental Patagonia. In other words, from the center of Argentina to the End of the World.

The pioneers who came together to bring at once a large number of animals will be divided into two different Estancias. Anyway, this trip will be beneficial for both of this businesses. These pioneers were foreigners and their names were: Henry Jamieson, John Hamilton, Jack MacLean, and Thomas Saunders. One Australian, one Scotsman and two englishmen.

These men started their enterprise in Buenos Aires where the four of them met. Then they went to Bahía Blanca by train (800 km south of Buenos Aires) where they began to visit the different farms in the area to buy animals, both horses and sheep.

Together with dogs they had brought from Punta Arenas, they began to move slowly towards Río Colorado, the virtual frontier and gateway to Patagonia from the north.

They crossed this river and were joined by some *gauchos* and a Tehuelche Indian who knew the way and who would be the guide for the long journey. It was important to know where to find water and good places to stop along the way.

Jamieson was "the boss" and he lived for many years in the South Island of New Zealand before, where he worked in sheep farms near Mount Cook, in a region similar to Patagonia.

Saunders, Hamilton and MacLean also had experience, but only that gained in the Falkland Islands, while Jamieson was years ahead of them.

In total there were eleven men who started writing this Patagonian epic.

Please refer to the map on page 104 to follow references.

Start of the Great Sheep Drive: Rio Negro Territory

In September 1888, 11 men, 5,000 sheep, 500 horses, and approximately 20 dogs set out from northern Patagonia in the Rio Negro Territory with the aim of reaching Rio Gallegos, the capital of the Santa Cruz Territory.

The group was organized as follows: at the front were the horses, of which there were 500, and in their marching, they marked the track that the giant sheep herd should follow. And closing the group were the *pilcheros,* who were in charge of riding the toughest horses that carried the load.

The men spent the whole day apart, while they met at the end of the day with the *pilcheros* who were in charge of making the meal, usually with the game of the day or some sheep that had to be butchered for some reason.

The dogs had to be tied up to avoid fights, and the meat was then divided among all the participants in the hard work.

Each man carried leather mats that would be used to lie down and sleep under the Patagonian skies, hoping in that discomfort, to find the energy to carry on a new day's work as soon as the sun rose.

During each day's marches it was estimated that the whole group was almost 1.5 kilometers long, so when stops were made on hot days, an allowance had to be made for waiting for those who were further behind.

At times it was possible to go up to a week without seeing water, and the water reserves were carried by the *pilcheros*. The bags were made of guanaco skin, although after several days the water began to have an unpleasant taste.

A sheep drive in Patagonia.
Photograph kindly shared by Luis Quezada.

Crossing the rivers was the main challenge: the most important thing was to make sure that the animals did not cross on their own and unsupervised, because if one crosses, they will all cross because they follow each other. Identifying the best place to do it is critical, as many rivers have narrow areas that allow the animals to swim across. And in other cases, it was necessary to use basic barges or rafts.

The animals, often when they need water, can sense it in the distance and naturally rush into the rivers. But considering the size of this group, they had to be organized so that they could get close to the rushing Patagonian rivers to drink water and avoid any unwanted accidents.

Arriving at the first large stream, called Valcheta, this group of men lost about 50 animals and a dog in the maneuver for these reasons. The skins and meat of the animals that died on the road were sold along the way.

At Valcheta, the party came across Tehuelche Indians who were on a journey and happened to camp nearby. It was feared that they might want to steal animals, but according to the writings, Jamieson and MacLean made themselves understood and made a favorable exchange of sheepskins for some food and help in skirting the stream.

As previously mentioned, the Tehuelches were nomadic and lived by hunting choique and guanaco, and since the arrival of the white man in those latitudes they were already accustomed to exchange. Some of them were even fluent in Spanish.

In the Territory of Chubut (1888-1889)

Sometime later, on the way to the Chubut, both men and animals began to suffer from the lack of water. A group of geese appeared and the guide of the group, an Indian, commented that it was necessary to follow them, as they knew where there was water and grass. One of the men in the group set out to follow them and that same night they would make camp near a thawing pond. The guide's knowledge has saved the expedition in several occasions.

During one night they heard barking and, just when they thought everything was going well, they realized that one or more pumas had killed about 20 animals. This was hard news for the pioneers who had invested so much money in the animals. Once again, faced with the loss, they returned to hunt the animals.

They were now close to reaching a small settlement: the Welsh colony of Chubut. This colony is of great historical value to Patagonia, and we will devote a chapter to them later in this book.

They spent almost 3 months with them, where they rented fields for grazing the animals and completed the shearing of the animals, which in this case would be done with scissors. The bales of wool will be sold and the trip will continue only in autumn, when the strength of the Chubut River decreases, because in midsummer the snowmelt brings a lot of water from the Andes.

The group will spend perhaps their best days there, sleeping indoors and eating food made from a variety of vegetables, as well as learning about Welsh culture and participating in Welsh festivities.

When the river's flow dropped in March 1889, the protagonists had to assemble a raft by hand to cross the Chubut River; it took them about two weeks between horses and sheep whose numbers had swelled to almost 600 equines and 6,000 sheep.

The winter of 1889 found them marching slowly and far from the sea, but skirting the Chico River, the only source of safe and constant water for the longest stretch of the drive that lay ahead. They were fortunate to find some estancias along the way that welcomed them with joy and surprise at having visitors at such an inhospitable time of year. Hail is not that common, but some time it happens. When hail caught the group marching, the men covered themselves with sea lion hides. These were also acquired in the Welsh colony.

The next objective was to reach an Estancia in Puerto Deseado, where friends of John Hamilton, whose relationship had begun in the Malvinas, were waiting for them.

Summer of 1890 and arrival in Santa Cruz Territory

The friends of Hamilton accomodated the group and in December 1889, they carried out a second shearing, this time with state-of-the-art technology for that time, using hydraulic machines for the work. They have sheared the animals in 10 days and produced about 12,000 kilos of wool which, packed in about 600 bales, was exported directly to Europe.

Leaving Puerto Deseado, they continued their march through the Territory of Santa Cruz, where their destination was south of the Rio Gallegos, at Estancia Punta Loyola.

To entertain themselves, the gauchos ran horse races where they placed bets. When they were bored, they gave names to the sheep and talked to them along the way.

The last great challenge for this group would be to cross the wide Santa Cruz River, which we have already discussed from Darwin's and Moreno's expeditions. Here they had to hire the services of rafters, who helped them to successfully cross the river ("success" means losing a few animals on the way - and in this crossing the losses were only 25 animals). There, in the area of Puerto Santa Cruz, they also sold sheep and horse hides, which they exchanged for jerky beef, drinks, tobacco, and some money.

In this last part of the journey, they suffered the theft of animals by the Tehuelche Indians of the area. Fortunately they were able to solve it by talking to the cacique who disapproved of this type of attitude and ordered the immediate return of the animals. In any case, Jamieson decided to give some animals as a reward to the Tehuelches who returned the stolen goods.

Herding sheep in a Patagonian Estancia.
Photograph kindly shared by Luis Quezada.

They finally arrived in June 1880 at their final destination: Río Gallegos, capital of the Territory of Santa Cruz where the four foreigners intended to exploit their Estancias. Two years crossing the unknown Patagonia to be able to build a future on the animals they herded to such a distant destination.

The protagonists of this story managed to arrive with almost the same number of animals, between births and deaths along the journey: approximately 5,000 sheep and 500 horses.

This "Great Sheep Drive" was not an isolated case, as there will be more. But this great first journey left literally a great mark on the terrain that would later be used by other groups. What they discovered along the way, such as ravines, lagoons, and other geographical features, encouraged other immigrants to seek land in Patagonia, attracting mainly settlers from the Falklands, given the close relations that linked them with the protagonists.

It is worth mentioning that wool was Argentina's main export for more than forty years. By 1888, only 300,000 sheep were counted in Patagonia, but by 1930 it was home to 16 million animals.

I hope I have detailed the vicissitudes of these men as fairly as possible, for the diary kept by Henry Jamieson was lost and never found. What we are left with are some books that rescue the oral accounts of the pioneers and descendants of pioneers who still make Patagonia their home today. This is the case with the work of Pedro Dobrée, whose lines inspired this chapter.

Lighthouse Les Eclaireurs near Ushuaia, Tierra del Fuego (AR)
Many times is wrongly called the "Lighthouse at the end of the world".
Photo from the autor.

CHAPTER 12

Tierra del Fuego

We have already read about different events that took place in Patagonia, such as the Conquest of the Desert, the border problems with Chile and the arrival of immigrants who began to settle in ranches known as Estancias.

In this chapter, I will focus on Tierra del Fuego and will also mention other particularities, given its very southern location. I will begin by recounting some generalities that will help to understand the relationship between Tierra del Fuego and the events mentioned so far in the book .

When we talk about Tierra del Fuego, we are talking about Patagonia. It is important to make this clear, because geographically it has a different aspect from the mainland Patagonia we have been talking about. Its history also has some very interesting milestones to mention.

General

Tierra del Fuego is an island located between the Strait of Magellan and Cape Horn. Its name comes from Magellan's voyage, where he describes that from its coasts large amounts of fires could be seen.

Thanks to its name, it aroused the fascination of sailors of the time and confirmed their suspicions by presenting a landscape of forest, mountains, fire and ice. It was also seen as dangerous by the large number of shipwrecks that occurred in its vicinity. All this generated a romanticism about its name, and the adventure that lay ahead for travelers sailing in such southern waters.

Old map of Tierra del Fuego.
Author: Charles Furlong Wellington (1917) Public Domain.

The landscape

As in all Patagonia, the wind is a determining factor to know its landscape. But you must take into account something else: the Andes Mountains play a decisive role in Tierra del Fuego.

As in continental (or mainland) Patagonia, in Tierra del Fuego there are the two ecosystems mentioned as steppe and forest, but to know where to find them, we must know how the mountains influence this sector.

The Cordillera de los Andes extends from North to South throughout the American continent but in Tierra del Fuego, the direction of the mountain range runs from West to East. This generates a natural dividing line that gives us a steppe landscape in the northern part of the island. While in the southern part of the island we will find the presence of the forest. This native forest is also composed of the Nothofagus family.

Forest near Ushuaia.
Source: "Terra do Fogo" por Miradas.com.br under license CC BY 2.0

The *fauna* of the island:

It is important to mention that the puma is not present in Tierra del Fuego, and this leaves the terrain for the guanaco and the fox, which are the largest animals here.

Being Tierra del Fuego an island, the marine fauna is of great importance, with the presence of whales and sea lions for the most part. This attracted from the 1800s onwards a large number of hunting ships seeking to supply the important countries of the northern hemisphere with blubber and oil for illumination. Thus, a large number of species suffered, or were on the verge of extinction.

Many penguin colonies also make their home on the coasts and small islands in the area. They were also once hunted.

Talking about birds, the presence of the Andean Condor with its 3-meter wingspan rivals that of the Black-browed Albatross. The Condor is the largest continental bird in the world, while the Albatross family includes the largest bird species in the world.

Curiously, in the 20th century, the government of Tierra del Fuego introduced beavers with the idea of developing the fur industry. It is said that they brought beavers from Canada and, seeing that their fur did not adapt to the climate, they had to abandon the project, leaving them in the wild and causing serious changes to the island's ecosystem.

The first settlers

In Tierra del Fuego alone there were 4 tribes, two of them were nomadic guanaco hunters like the *Selk 'nam* (also known as Onas) and *Haush*. Living surrounded by water, they also made use of molluscs and animals that washed up on their shores. But their way of life revolved around chasing guanacos.

The other two tribes were the only canoe tribes in the Patagonian region. In other words, their way of life depended on the sea and what it provided. Their diet also consisted of shellfish, but they lived by hunting marine fauna such as sea lions. Whale strandings were a major event in the life of the canoeists of Tierra del Fuego.

Unfortunately, these Fuegian tribes also suffered the impacts of the white man on their territory: most of the Europeans who arrived were religious people who tried to evangelize the natives and change their way of life. Let us rememeber f Fitz Roy kidnapping natives as well in the first trip the HMS Beagle. Moreover, it has been reported many times that families of natives were kidnapped and taken to Europe to be exhibited in zoos. There are photographs proving these facts in France, Germany, and Switzerland. The most curious thing is that they were presented as "cannibals", which is not true. But the lack of interest in studying them, coupled with an interest in making a profit, allowed this inaccurate fact to go unnoticed.

Yámanas in Cape Horn, 1883. Possibly dressed by missioners.
Source: Archivo General de la Nación Argentina AGN_DDF Caja 2508, Inv: 350178.

The "Conquest of the Desert" took place exclusively in mainland Patagonia, i.e. up to the Strait of Magellan.

The island of Tierra del Fuego did not receive military troops from this campaign, i.e. the argentine government did not act directly in the territory of Tierra del Fuego. But genocides did take place here too, silently as mentioned in the atrocious examples mentioned before.

Today, in Tierra del Fuego there is an attempt to vindicate the native people, with much effort being put into research, publications, museums, and giving back to the places on the island the names given to them by the original settlers.

Ushuaia, the name of the present city, in *Yaghan* (Yámana language), means "bay that penetrates towards the sunset".

Onashaga, was the native name for the now known Beagle Channel.

The border between Argentina and Chile in Tierra del Fuego

We already know the events that took place between Argentina and Chile regarding the border in continental Patagonia: the first treaty of "peace and friendship", with the difference of positions that led to international arbitration. There, with the figure of Perito Moreno as the protagonist, a worrying issue in the Cordillera area was resolved.

But what about Tierra del Fuego? Arbitration did not take place here, as the boundaries had been fixed in the 1881 agreement and sealed in the famous "Embrace of the Strait" between both presidents.

In Tierra del Fuego, an imaginary line was drawn from Cape Espiritu Santo at latitude 52° 40' southwards, coinciding with the western Greenwich meridian, 68° 34', until it touched the Beagle Channel. Tierra del Fuego is Chilean in its western part and Argentine in its eastern part.

This is quite explanatory: for this reason, there is an arbitrary line that cuts Tierra del Fuego in half.

Map of Tierra del Fuego.
"Mapa antiguo de Tierra del Fuego, Patagonia (old map of Tierra del Fuego, Patagonia)." by thejourney1972 (South America addicted) under license CC BY 2.0

But the text of the Tierra del Fuego agreement remains as it is:

"As for the islands, the Isla de los Estados, the islets immediately adjacent to it, and the other islands in the Atlantic to the east of Tierra del Fuego and the eastern coasts of Patagonia shall belong to the Argentine Republic, and all the islands south of the Beagle Channel as far as Cape Horn and those to the west of Tierra del Fuego shall belong to Chile".

What does this last part mean?

Isla de los Estados is an island just a few kilometers east of the coast of Tierra del Fuego (see map above). The other islands in the Atlantic, one might suppose, are the Falkland Islands and all the islands that, to the east, approach Antarctica. But was this really the case?

This deserves a separate chapter.

Arrival of the first Europeans in Tierra del Fuego

The first white men to come from Europe were missionaries. Tierra del Fuego was like a promised land for the missionaries who sought to evangelize and educate the natives of those distant territories, in order to convert them to the new faith, civilize them, and insert them socially into Western civilisation.

The most important missions were Anglican and Salesian.

The intention of the missionaries was to save the souls of the natives and also to change their customs that were considered savage, including nudity. Such was the vision of the time.

The first missionaries were of English origin, and initially settled in the Falkland Islands, where they lived for many years acclimatizing to the terrain. From there they made a base to approach Tierra del Fuego.

The founder and first secretary of the Missionary Society was Captain Allen Gardiner, who died of starvation in 1851 on an island in the Beagle Channel, waiting for a supply ship from England. The society was formed for the purpose of recruiting, sending, and supporting Christian missionaries to South America to evangelize the natives.

Later, the great protagonist of the first stable settlement in Tierra del Fuego was Thomas Bridges. He was an Anglican reverend who lived among the natives for several years, and managed to write a Yámana-English dictionary of about 20,000 words.

He settled in Ushuaia's Bay until the arrival of the Argentine government in 1884, when the city was founded. The Argentine government decided to give him 20,000 hectares so that he could settle and he founded the first estancia in Tierra del Fuego on the shores of the Beagle Channel. There, with several natives he took for his protection, he began his life as a rancher, leaving behind his religious life.

Estancia Harberton was the first Estancia in Tierra del Fuego. I had the good fortune to work here between 2006 and 2009 and it is a place where one can breathe living history and enjoy an enchanting landscape. One cannot imagine having chosen this location in the 19th century to settle with his family literally at the end of the world. An interesting book about this family and their life in Tierra del Fuego is called "*The uttermost part of the Earth*" by Lucas Bridges. Today, descendants of the Bridges family still run the establishment.

In any case, these types of evangelizing actions should be reviewed with different eyes today. Many of them provided humanitarian services, but with objectives and actions that transgress rights that today are universal. These missions assumed that the natives were completely alien to the right way, to Western life, and that they were doing them a favor by teaching them the new practices of the civilized world.

Gold Rush:

There was in Patagonia, and precisely in Tierra del Fuego, a first event that sparked people's interest in going to this remote place, and it was not precisely the easy access to the land. The land hid in some corners the presence of a valuable mineral: gold.

One of the best-known characters surrounding the stories of gold in Tierra del Fuego was a Romanian engineer named Julius Popper. According to his studies, he was able to determine that the chances of finding gold deposits in Tierra del Fuego must be very high, and when the news reached Buenos Aires, a frenzy broke out that led numerous entrepreneurs to travel south.

The increase of the population in Ushuaia was driven by this "gold rush" that began in 1886 and lasted until the early 1900s. This forgotten corner of Patagonia received a large new population that found itself in a territory still inhabited by natives, which unfortunately triggered violent encounters between the two sides.

These gold prospectors lived in a very basic way, setting up tents or building wooden huts covered with earth to insulate them from the cold. Gold panning was done between spring and autumn because of the milder climate and longer daylight hours.

The characters who came to look for gold in Tierra del Fuego were very heterogeneous, but they had one thing in common: greed. Although they worked together, they jealously guarded the gold collected to avoid robbery. Many times, they buried the loot and when the thief was discovered, they ended up in a somewhat bloody event.

People kept arriving, although the amount of gold to be found might not be worth the trip. Perhaps the rumors were deliberately exaggerated to attract people to Ushuaia.

What we can say is that it was only a "fever" that lasted a few years and made a few people rich. For example, Julius Popper was able to acquire land near the gold-rich areas, where he was able to mint gold coins with his name on them, which sparked controversy in the region. Curiously, Julius Popper died at the age of 36 at his home in Buenos Aires.

Julius Popper made his own gold coins in Tierra del Fuego, 1889.
Autor: Julius Popper (1857-1893) Public Domain via Wikimedia.

Estancias in Tierra del Fuego

Following the phenomenon of the Estancias that took place in mainland Patagonia, the island of Tierra del Fuego was no exception.

Sheep farming was also the main reason for the occupation of the island and, with the late arrival of the Argentine government, it meant a late planning of its colonization. That resulted in very few immigrants to this island.

In Tierra del Fuego all exploitable land was used for wool production, the product of which was sent to Buenos Aires or directly to Europe.

Something we must highlight is the presence of two ranchers who began to get rich thanks to land hoarding. They were José Menéndez and Mauricio Braun.

José Menéndez was a Spaniard who built an empire in Patagonia based in Punta Arenas. He was dedicated to the salvage of shipwrecks, he had general stores, he had ships that communicated with Patagonia, and finally he had a lot of land. In his mansion he was able to host the Argentinian president Julio Roca during the events of the signing of the peace treaty in 1881 on the Magellan Strait. In this way, he made himself known to both nations. Later, with some lobbying, he was able to acquire huge tracts of land in Argentinean and Chilean Patagonia and Tierra del Fuego.

In other words, most of the Estancias often belonged not to immigrants who came in search of a dream, but to unscrupulous, greedy landowners who took advantage of their position to get richer and richer.

José Menéndez Menéndez (born in Miranda, Avilés, Asturias, Spain; Nov. 2nd, 1846-deceased in Buenos Aires, Argentina; April, 24th 1918) Spanish businessman that had great influence in the Patagonian region.
Image: Unknown author ca. 1900, via Wikimedia Commons

In Tierra del Fuego alone, Menéndez managed approximately 1,000,000 hectares. Later we will talk about Menéndez and other landowners, and the inequality of opportunities they generated in the Patagonian territory.

But the big problem in Tierra del Fuego was the lack of population. That is to say, there were plenty of Estancias. But there were no towns or cities, except for port cities like Rio Grande or Ushuaia. In the next chapter, we will see how Ushuaia managed to begin a gradual increase in terms of population.

Lighthouse at San Juan de Salvamento Bay.
This is the real "Lighthouse at the End of the World" on Isla de los Estados, Tierra del Fuego, Argentina.
Photo kindly shared by Carlos Vairo, director from Museo Marítimo and Museo del Presidio de Ushuaia.

CHAPTER 13

The prison and the lighthouse at the End of the World

The "end of the world" - this was the historical nickname given by the sailors to the southern waters of Patagonia. Especially if we talk about Tierra del Fuego and this archipelago that bids farewell to the American continent in the vicinity of the South Pole. This reference awakened the hopes, challenges and fantasies of those who ventured to visit these lands.

To speak of "the end of the world" is to speak of a geographical circumstance that applies a poetic romanticism to these marginal places and gives a quota of drama to each story set in this place so far south of the planet.

Therefore, in this chapter we will talk about two places that have been attributed this exceptional characteristic given their location. The stories in this chapter are twofold: we will talk about the "Lighthouse of the end of the world" - which for many lives on in Jules Verne's novel. And we will also talk about the "Prison at the End of the World" which operated in these latitudes and which today can be visited as a museum in the present-day city of Ushuaia in the south of Tierra del Fuego.

The aim is to continue the story of the previous chapter and to clarify how a place like Ushuaia was able to increase its population in such an isolated place.

Idea of the penal colony

Successful examples of penal colonies already existed in the world.

France had a penal colony in New Caledonia and another in Algeria, while England had a penal colony in Australia in present-day Sydney. Argentina had begun to conceive this idea after the border agreements with Chile, and at this time Tierra del Fuego was identified as an appropriate place to develop a penal establishment.

The main reason for a penal colony was to assert the sovereignty of a marginal territory by settling an effective population.

Ushuaia (capital city of Tierra del Fuego) was founded in 1884, and the first prisoners who arrived in these latitudes did not settle here, but on Isla de los Estados (Staten Island). This island is located 24 km off the east coast of Tierra del Fuego and was chosen for the installation of a lighthouse and a sub-prefecture of the Argentine navy. The prisoners were chosen for their skills, as they had to help in the installation of this official settlement in such a hostile place as the aforementioned island.

Don't be confused: Tierra del Fuego is an island, the largest one. And Isla de los Estados is another, much smaller island just east of Tierra del Fuego. (See map of previous chapter)

Isla de los Estados has a mountainous appearance and the average annual temperature of the island is 2° C (or 35° Farenheit) and it is surrounded by a sea that also has a similar temperature.

There are few large land animals, mostly rodents and rabbits. Penguins and sea lions are also found on the island.

Interestingly, there were quite a few women accompanying the soldiers and prisoners who lived in this remote place. The prison was located there between 1884 and 1889 in the bay of San Juan de Salvamento and had about 50 prisoners. Its precarious conditions led to its transfer for humanitarian reasons.

The Lighthouse at the End of the World

In these southern waters, danger lurks in every storm. The Argentine navy had installed a lighthouse on the Isla de los Estados in the bay of San Juan de Salvamento to guide sailors and help them navigate these rough seas. The navy had placed this light there on a salvage mission for possible shipwrecks, which were very numerous in the region.

The name "Lighthouse at the End of the World" positions this lighthouse as the last light before the unknown Antarctica.

According to Carlos Pedro Vairo - director of the Museum of the End of the World, and writer of several history books - Jules Verne's novel "The Lighthouse at the End of the World" is based on this lighthouse installed on the Isla de los Estados. Although many claim that Jules Verne never visited the place, Vairo patiently explains all the coincidences between the novel and the reality of the place. The dimensions of the island described in the book are very approximate, the events that take place in the book also happened (escape of prisoners) and the Argentine ship is called Santa Fe in his book, when in real life, the ship was the Parana (river on the shores of the city of Santa Fe). Vairo insists that somehow the stories of the southern waters reached Jules Verne's ears.

I recommend the works of Carlos Pedro Vairo for those who want to know more about this southern region.

Some time later, Argentina joined other European nations in collaborating in expeditions to Antarctica. This agreement was signed in 1899, and our country undertook to provide direct support to the cause by installing magnetic observatories. This new establishment came about as a result of a request from the *Royal Geographical Society of London* to the Argentine government to collaborate with the International Commission for the Antarctic Expedition. For this purpose, the construction of a magnetic observatory and various meteorological installations were required.

This new lighthouse, which accompanied the observatory of Isla Observatorio, took over the duties of the one at San Juan de Salvamento taking over in 1902 the fame of being "the lighthouse at the end of the world": the last light before traveling to the uncharted polar waters.

This is the only photo of the San Juan de Salvamento lighthouse and prisoner stables from 1898 taken by Adrian de Gerlache's "BELGICA" expedition.
Photos kindly shared by Carlos Vairo, director from Museo Marítimo and Museo del Presidio de Ushuaia.

Moving from the prison to Ushuaia

After the prison on Isla de los Estados was closed, in 1902 it was decided to move the prison to Ushuaia, which at that time had a stable population of less than 200 people.

Prisoners took advantage of the transfer to escape, some of them succeeded, and others were recaptured. Imagine in such a lonely and remote place, escape is no easy task.

For the then small town of Ushuaia the arrival of the prison had an important commercial impact. It was already very busy with the arrival of ships, gold prospectors, and also because of the Estancias in the region.

This prison had several buildings, but the one that survives today began to be built in 1902. The construction was carried out with local materials and with the labor of the prisoners, who had been placed in temporary prisons. The building has 5 pavilions with 76 exterior cells each. They totaled 380 single-person cells measuring 1.50 by 2 meters, with a thick wooden door with a glazed hole one meter above the ground that allowed for surveillance from the outside. Ventilation came through a 20 x 20 cm latticed opening near the ceiling. A real solitary and absolute confinement.

The 5 wards converged radially to a "multiple rotunda", where all the prisoners were concentrated for different purposes: to go to different tasks both inside and outside the prison, such as conference room, mass, auditorium and cinema. This was to keep an eye on the prisoners when they were in their cells.

The employees of the prison

We want to know how Ushuaia grew, and here the prison and the job opportunities it provided as an institution play a fundamental role. The employees lived in the city and, as the prison grew, so did its population: families arrived to accompany each new prison employee, and in turn, new shops opened to supply the new arrivals. Many Spaniards, Italians, Chileans and also Croatians and Yugoslavs were part of the early citizenry.

Prisoners accessed a disciplinary system in which they had access to a small income for their work and often went around the city spending these small sums of money on some "treats" such as liquor, tobacco and food other than prison food.

By 1920 Ushuaia had a population of 1,000, of which just over half were convicts.

Ushuaia prison, the "prison at the end of the world" and the city in full growth.
Photo kindly shared by Carlos Vairo, director from Museo Marítimo and Museo del Presidio de Ushuaia.

The prisoners

The selection of those who were to be transferred to the prison at the end of the world in Ushuaia was very varied: at the beginning they were chosen for their manual skills, as in this first stage they were to help build the prison itself and the famous lighthouse we spoke of earlier.

Over time, the most dangerous prisoners were also brought in, such as serial murderers of the time and enemies of the state, mostly anarchists and extremists. In the same way, minors with minor offenses were sent to prison, but the ones that lived on the streets, they were eligible to serve their sentences in Ushuaia. It was said to help prevent these young people from falling into the vices of Buenos Aires and to help them get their lives back on track.

There were many famous prisoners, although few of international renown. A legend says that Carlos Gardel, the famous tango singer of the early 20th century passed through this prison. Some correspondence would be proof that Gardel, when he was a minor, was sent to serve a short sentence in Ushuaia, but nothing of this is verified in the penitentiary archives: perhaps someone wanted to prevent the record from tarnishing the image of one of the most brilliant idols of Argentine culture.

Disciplinary system

The prison had workshops such as shoemaking, tailoring, carpentry, a pasta factory, laundry and more. There was also a fire brigade, a brass band, a library with more than 1000 books, a school, a pharmacy, and electric power.

The prison's services were made accessible to the entire city of Ushuaia, which, thanks to the prison, also had a telephone line. The prison workshops had the dual mission of training prisoners and providing services to the city of Ushuaia. The prisoners enjoyed a disciplinary system of paid work and, through their work, could save money to spend or send home for family support.

The town of Ushuaia, as we have said, benefited from the transfer of this prison: the convicts were able to lay out the streets and erect buildings and bridges. For the inhabitants of Ushuaia, the coexistence with the convicts was something usual, but for the visitors it was something quite striking at that time.

Tailoring workshop in the prison of Ushuaia.
Photo courtesy of Carlos Vairo, director of the Museo Marítimo y Museo del Presidio de Ushuaia.

Carpentry workshop at the Presidio of Ushuaia.
Photo courtesy of Carlos Vairo, director of the Museo Marítimo y Museo del Presidio de Ushuaia.

Curious photograph of a theatrical presentation in the prison.
Photo courtesy of Carlos Vairo, Director of the Museo Marítimo y Museo del Presidio de Ushuaia.

Work related to the prison sawmill.
Photo courtesy of Carlos Vairo, Director of the Museo Marítimo y Museo del Presidio de Ushuaia.

The sawmill

Prisoners with good behavior were chosen for outdoor work in the vicinity of Mount Susana, where the sawmill that supplied the prison and the city of Ushuaia with timber was located. Many of these prisoners preferred to work outdoors, regardless of the weather conditions, doing this strenuous work. For many of them it was the best way to kill time so that their sentences would pass as quickly as possible.

Monte Susana is a slope far from the center of the village, so a *xylocarril*, which is a train that travels on wooden tracks, was built. On this train the prisoners went to and from Monte Susana to carry out their work. And didn't they try to escape? Of course, but they were quickly caught or else they gave themselves up, because the bad weather, the lack of food, and the cold did not allow their mission to succeed. By simply lighting a fire, this would give them away.

The closure of the prison:

By the end of the 1930s the prison did not have a good reputation: cases of torture, political prisoners of a military dictatorship, and concealment of information on obscure issues marked the end of an institution that was the mainstay of the town of Ushuaia.

On 21 March 1947, invoking humanitarian reasons, the definitive closure of the prison was ordered, which caused great repercussions in Argentine society. The prisoners were transferred to other prisons in the country, concluding with the evacuation in 1949.

With the departure of the convicts, the town was suddenly empty, which was reflected in the deterioration of the houses, gardens and farms where they worked. It is calculated that, between those who left the prison and their families, approximately four thousand people left the island, practically half of the town by that time.

In 1950, the facilities were transferred to the Ministry of the Navy, so that with the arrival of the new families belonging to the Navy, a new chapter in the history of the settlement of Ushuaia was opened.

Ushuaia today:

For me, Ushuaia is one of the most interesting cities in Argentina because it is the southernmost city, but also because it is the only trans-Andean city in our country. I was there between 2006 and 2009 working, and I learned a lot about the history of the island. Those of us who live in Buenos Aires don't learn the history of these places at school.

Since 1990, this National Territory of Tierra del Fuego was declared a province under the name "*Tierra del Fuego, Antártida e Islas del Atlántico Sur*" (Tierra del Fuego, Antarctica and South Atlantic islands). With respect to its name, this Argentine province includes places whose sovereignty is in dispute, such as the Falklands, South Georgia, South Sandwich Islands, South Orkney Islands, South Shetland Islands, and Antarctica.

Ushuaia is the gateway to Antarctica: we are here only 1,000 kilometers away from the Antarctic Peninsula and today numerous cruise ships depart from the port of Ushuaia.

To say the least, it is curious that Antarctica is mentioned as a territory belonging to one country, but the South Atlantic islands are an active claim of the Argentine Republic seeking to recover historical and geographical sovereignty over the above-mentioned islands.

In the next chapter we will review the close relationship between Patagonia and Antarctica and some historical details of this frozen continent.

Antarctica
Photo courtesy of Ignacio Cánepa.

CHAPTER 14

Antarctica : beyond the End of the World

In the previous chapters we learned about the history of the last Argentinean extension in South America, which corresponds to Tierra del Fuego. The southernmost tip of the American continent, however, is Chilean and consists of Cape Horn. It is here that the largest number of shipwrecks in the world have been recorded. Mainly pirates and privateers used this southern route for smuggling to avoid the Strait of Magellan.

From Ushuaia to the Antarctic Peninsula is only about 1,000 kilometers, approximately 3 days of sailing, and today it is very common to find tourist cruises that make tours of the area. But in this chapter, we will talk about those who have been to Antarctica in the past, the activities they carried out, and the territorial claims that exist over this continent.

Today we all know that Antarctica is a sanctuary that does not belong to any country. The bases that exists on Antarctica are strictly scientific and that there is no economic exploitation of any kind (except for tourism). Personally, I have not been to Antarctica, and it is a dream to get to know these extreme latitudes. Living in Ushuaia in my youth, I remember being able to smell the ice thousands of kilometers away, pushed by the winds from the south. It only remains for me to invite you to read this chapter in order to discover some historical curiosities of this place and the close relationship between Argentine Patagonia and Antarctica.

Antarctica: general aspects

If anyone reading this chapter has been to Antarctica, they will know that these lines are written from the objectivity of the technical data of this place.

Antarctica is a continent with an area slightly smaller than the size of Russia, with the great peculiarity that there is a thick mass of ice covering it. This ice sheet can be up to two kilometers thick at times. It is considered a large semi-arid steppe, as rainfall is low, and in a solid state. The white monotony is broken by the rocky outcrops that occur mostly on the Antarctic Peninsula, which is the continent's most important geographical feature. There are also two mountain ranges, and the mountain peaks that outcrop above the ice are known as *nunatak*. The mountains here are a continuation of the Andes Mountains that give rise to the aforementioned South Atlantic islands of South Georgia, South Sandwich Islands, South Orkney, South Shetland, and the Antarctic Peninsula.

There is no indigenous population, and plant life is limited to mosses and lichens that make use of the bare ice soils. Animals are migratory, such as flying birds (skuas, gulls, cormorants) and flightless birds such as penguins.

The penguin is a flightless bird species that lives in the southern hemisphere only. They live between the sea and the land and use the land for nesting during the mating season. I recommend here to watch the National Geographic documentary called *The March of the Penguins*.

Other important animals are amphibious mammals such as seals, sea lions, and elephant seals, as well as the presence of whales in these southern waters whose general food for life is krill.

There are rivers, but not as we usually know them. We are talking about rivers of ice, or rather glaciers. In this respect, the first close relationship between Antarctica and Patagonia lies in the glacial ice. Antarctica is undoubtedly the largest ice mass on Earth. Secondly, Greenland, which has another large mass of ice covering our planet. And thirdly, in Patagonia, is the Southern Patagonian Ice Field. This ice field lies in the southern part of the Andes Mountains and is safeguarded in its entirety by Argentina and Chile, which, with three national parks, protect this incredible world heritage site.

The first sailors: pirates and hunters

At the beginning of the book, we talked about the importance of Magellan's expedition that discovered the Strait that bears his name: it was also the expedition that went furthest south until then, around the year 1520.

Over time, this southern sea became populated by ships trying to break the trade monopoly that existed in South America. This monopoly forced the colonies of the time to trade with the corresponding crown, in this case Spain or Portugal. It was at this time that the southern waters began to be populated by pirates and privateers who, in order to avoid controls, smuggled contraband through the Drake's Passage, a water passage between South America and Antarctica, precisely between Cape Horn and the Antarctic Peninsula. This is where the new approaches begin.

The big challenge was the strong storms in the region, which often pushed the ships to dock at the various islands mentioned above. The Georgias, Sandwich, Orkney and South Shetland Islands were discovered by chance. Most of them have English names, as Britain succeeded Spain in the domination of the seas after 1700.

In Antarctica there is a rather special phenomenon known as the katabatic winds that provides a system of winds blowing from the South Pole out to sea. This phenomenon has pushed and prevented ships from those early times from approaching the mysterious continent. The unfavorable winds, the frozen sea, the harsh climate, and the lack of naval advances, prevented the discovery of this white continent.

From the Patagonian coasts and southwards, historically, large populations of seals, sea lions, and elephant seals were found. Naturally, and from what has been explained so far in the book, these latitudes were secret, inhospitable lands, where there were no laws due to the lack of effective control. In these places man found the motivation to move further and further south. But not to enrich the geography, but to enrich himself. This would mean that for many years that islands, geographical features and important maritime notations were kept under strict secrecy from unscrupulous hunters who wanted to protect their source of wealth. Gradually, these places were to become rustic hunters' settlements.

Hunting of seals, sea lions and elephant seals (1770-1830)

The importance of fur seals, sea lions and elephant seals decided the fate of these southern waters. The fur trade with the East was very important and there seemed to be no end to the wealth of the southern waters. The images of the hunting of these marine mammals are utterly heartless and require unscrupulous people to carry out these bloody deeds. With their holds full of salted skins and hides, these ships would return to a safe port, such as Buenos Aires, where these precious goods would be re-shipped to Europe or Asia. More important was the secrecy of the location of the hunting grounds. To make public the information of these places would result in the loss of the "monopoly" of such grounds. But keeping such a secret is not easy: sooner or later the information was passed from crew to crew and this resulted in massive predation of the pelagic wealth of the South Seas.

Unfortunately, the indiscriminate and uncontrolled hunting of these animals brought these species to the brink of extinction.

Current Antarctic fauna.
Photo courtesy of Ignacio Cánepa.

Whaling activities in Antarctica (1850 - 1930)

A clarification: whaling is not something new. It has been in our DNA for 10,000 years in the northern hemisphere and over the years this kind of activity has evolved. But when I talk about evolution, unfortunately there is nothing positive about it. What evolved was, of course, the technology applied to this activity. But what also evolved was the greed that surrounded this practice, which became very lucrative. The importance of whale blubber and whale oil for lighting, candles and soap had become a very lucrative business, as we can see in the novel Moby Dick.

Whaling in the southern seas began shortly after the hunting of seals, sea lions and elephant seals, still with this secrecy that meant that information about these waters was transmitted in an intermittent and confusing way. The whale that lives in the south is the Blue Whale, among other species, which have the peculiarity that when they die, they sink immediately. These marine mammals are almost 20 meters long, and under these conditions, hunting was unfeasible. Perhaps if the hunt was close to the coast the chances increased, but what was also lacking was the zoological knowledge to get to know the animal better. When hunting and slaughtering the animal, it was impossible to carry out in-depth studies on these animals in these times when everything was a "trade secret".

The development of the harpoon gun was a breakthrough that brought more than positive results for Scandinavian companies in the northern seas. This caused an important decrease of the whale population in those waters. It also brought specimens closer to being studied from a zoological point of view, as the animal was harpooned and dragged entirely to the coast, where it was to be slaughtered.

Having exhausted this resource in the north, eyes turned to the south of the Earth.

At this time, as we have seen so far in the book, Argentina was seeking to position itself as a world power. Immigrants were arriving to work the land and unparalleled quantities of grain, meat and wool were being exported. Peace and border boundaries had been secured, and this attracted the attention of foreign companies looking to do business with the country. Argentina had an export profile and the extraction of wealth from our seas was more than interesting.

Whaling was a business that extended to the islands of the South Atlantic and Antarctica until about 1930. The South Georgia and South Orkney Islands, where whaling factories operated, are no longer a secret. The South Sandwich Islands did not have any establishments as the island does not have any repaired sites for settlement. Most of the whaling factories that operated in the region were English or Scandinavian until the economic crisis of 1930 affected the activity: prices fell sharply and the income was no longer interesting due to the high costs of the structure. The activity had a slight upturn with the appearance of factory ships.

In the 20th century, scientific studies proved that it was impossible to control reasonable levels of hunting of these marine mammals and, from 1931 onwards, hunting bans and strict protection of whale species began to be enacted, which only became general for all species in 1987. The whale, unfortunately, was brought to the brink of extinction worldwide.

William Speirs Bruce visiting Francisco Moreno.
Photo from Caras y Caretas Magazine n. 273.

Argentina and its presence in Antarctica since 1904

Argentina also joined the scientific activities and supported all the expeditions that landed in our country to travel to the unknown Antarctica. It was not until the beginning of the 20th century that the first scientific explorations began to arrive in Antarctica.

Perito Moreno, of whom we have already spoken in this book, had supported Argentina's efforts to be part of the polar outpost and to take part in the international geographic congresses held in Berlin and London. In these congresses the project of carrying out studies, observations and measurements in different parts of Antarctica was born. The aim was to share the result and analyse them together to establish the influence that the continent has on the rest of our planet, and also to improve geographic knowledge.

Later, thanks to Perito Moreno's contacts, our country received William Bruce: a professor with several polar voyages who had installed a small house where a meteorological observatory operated on Laurie Island (part of the South Orkney Islands). During his visit to Buenos Aires, this professor offered these facilities to the argentinean government, as it was unlikely that this professor would be able to continue with this measuring activity over time. On this occasion the Argentine government acquired the facilities offered by Professor Bruce thanks to the active intervention of the Argentine perito.

In January 1904, a group of men left Buenos Aires to take charge of the aforementioned facilities, sent off from the dock by Perito Moreno. They arrived at South Orkney in mid-February, almost 4 weeks later and during the first days, repair work was carried out to make the small house habitable. On February 22nd, 1904, an anemometer was installed putting this observatory into effective operation under the Argentine flag. The observations of this station began that day and continued uninterruptedly until the present day, giving greater precision to the meteorological forecasts of the South Atlantic.

Every 22nd of February, the day of the "Argentine presence in Antarctica" is commemorated.

Photograph of that day February 22, 1904. Courtesy Fundación Marambio.

Territorial claims in Antarctica

I said earlier that it was curious to think that someone would claim ownership of Antarctica, since today we assume that it is a continent that belongs to no one. Economic activities are prohibited on the continent. The only purpose of settlements in Antarctica should be scientific purposes. But this assertion today has only been achieved over time.

Many countries saw the economic and geostrategic advantages of this particular continent. Of course, the hostile nature of this environment delayed the arrival of man, who in spite of everything, took great pains to drive to extinction the animals mentioned before.

Lack of control and excessive greed were responsible for leaving this legacy in such extreme latitudes. But with the passing of time, and the vision of people with a conservationist sense, they were able to bend the trend so that what happened to these species would not be replicated on the continent, trying to position it as a sanctuary and not seek to exploit it economically.

In any case, acts of sovereignty have taken place in Antarctica since early in the 20th century: in these lines I told you how Argentina commemorates the day it began its permanent settlement in Antarctica. But it is not the only country with a territorial claim.

Seven nations have active claims to Antarctic territory: four are neighboring countries such as Argentina, Chile, Australia and New Zealand. Three other countries in the northern hemisphere also have claims: Britain (for its control over the Falklands and other South Atlantic islands), Norway (for the expedition that reached the South Pole in 1911) and France (for an expedition in 1840). All these claims are based on historical causes.

Was there tension between these countries? Of course there was. The claims are delimited by longitudinal lines that end at the South Pole. In the case of adjoining countries such as Argentina, the western and eastern end points of the country are used to project the longitudes towards the Pole demarcating their "Antarctic projection" forming something like a triangle, or a slice of cake.

Tensions escalated greatly during World War II and continued during the Cold War. In order to avoid conflicts that could target Antarctica and its resources, it was decided to sign an Antarctic Treaty between these 7 countries, to which almost 50 countries eventually adhered.

The Antarctic Treaty

The Antarctic Treaty was signed in 1959 in the United States and declares Antarctica a natural reserve dedicated to science and peace. Any activity with mineral resources is prohibited and an international committee is created to advise the adhering countries on environmental protection and conservation issues. This treaty is one of the longest-lasting treaties that has lasted without major problems. Of course, the seven countries with the claims in question signed happily, because it does not constitute a renunciation of any pre-1961 territorial claims - i.e. the pact froze existing territorial claims and established Antarctica as an international scientific reserve. It also prohibited nuclear testing and "any measures of a military character, except to assist scientific research".

Since then, 42 other nations have joined the Treaty, although only 29 - those with "substantial research activities" - have voting power and can make decisions on the present and future of Antarctica.

Since 1998 the Madrid Protocol has been in force, where members of the pact have agreed to continue to prohibit any non-scientific activity in Antarctica. The next review is in 2048 and who knows what will happen there. From what has been said in this chapter, let us hope that sanity prevails.

Antarctica does not belong to anyone, and hopefully it will continue to do so for a long time to come. But in this chapter, we have been able to see the close relationship between Argentina and this continent. Did you know that the Antarctic claim appears on Argentina's maps? Looks like this and is normally found on a corner of the map.

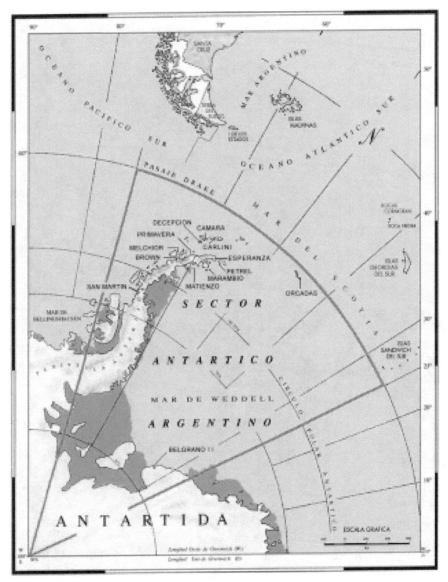

Portion of Antarctic territory claimed by Argentina: the extreme meridians of the country are used and projected towards the South Pole resulting in this "slice of cake" on the maps. *Courtesy Fundación Marambio.*

Welsh settlers opening the road between the Atlantic coast and the Andes mountain range.
Year 1899.
Unknown author. Public Domain.

CHAPTER 15

The Welsh colony in Patagonia (1865)

Much has already been said, but much is still unknown about Patagonia. One of the first great feats of its young modern history is the Welsh colonization of the valley of the Chubut River. The peculiarity of this colonization is that it took place before the already mentioned "Conquest of the Desert". This means that Patagonia still belonged to its original inhabitants living in the vastness of the steppe: the Tehuelches.

A group of 153 people from Wales were determined to land on the patagonian beaches to form a Welsh colony far from Britain. This small, almost unknown country was being absorbed politically, and they sought with this colonizing attempt to keep alive the personality of their people along with their language and customs.

Dear reader, let's walk together along the path of this colony: learning about its achievements and its failures in a land that is still wild and that Darwin described as "cursed".

The causes of Welsh exile

In Britain, with the arrival of the Anglo-Normans, a period of fighting began and ended with the subjugation of Wales in the 12th century. From then on there were no major changes for the Welsh, because by then, there were no things in Wales that were of interest to the British crown. Also because of the language barrier between English and Welsh.

Over time, the world changed, and the Industrial Revolution changed everyone's needs: coal was the main source of energy that powered the steam engine and was crucial in the iron and steel industry, for which iron was also highly prized.

At this time in the 19th century, interest in Wales increased because of the presence of iron and coal in its subsoil. Various parts of Wales had been industrialized. There were numerous foundries in the South Wales valleys, and coal mining spread widely across Wales.

Unfortunately, pressure from the British crown created an abusive capitalist monopoly over this population, whose quality of life declined drastically: misery and hunger were part of life with few prospects where even children worked in the mines. The religious and linguistic customs of the Welsh people were endangered by the economic and territorial appropriation that took place in these turbulent times.

It is here that the yearning of some of the inhabitants to somehow save their ancient culture was born and their language is considered their greatest exponent. The aim was to rescue these elements from the English advance with the creation of a Welsh Colony somewhere far away where they would not be intervened by any foreign influence. And that is where the opportunity of Patagonia came into the picture.

The idea of a Welsh colony in Patagonia

The first ideas of forming a Welsh colony in Patagonia came about at the beginning of the 20th century among a group of Welsh living in the United States. At that time there were a few associations of Welsh people living in this immense country after emigrating from Wales.

This initiative was of great interest, as they themselves had personally experienced the disadvantages of migrating alone in small groups. Living surrounded by other peoples was slowly leading them to lose their customs and language.

This problem was understood by Reverend Jones, who, after finishing his studies in the United States, traveled around visiting his compatriots who lived scattered throughout the country. There he saw how disorganized emigration led to the slow disappearance of their own customs, such as their unique language, which they had to lose in order to communicate better when meeting people of other nationalities.

Reverend Jones returned to Wales and worked on this idea with a number of people who were enthusiastic about taking this project forward. All agreed that Patagonia was the most appropriate place for the establishment of a colony. This was supported by the testimonies of Fitz Roy who had traveled the Patagonian coast in 1834 and had made good references to the valley of the Chubut River and the Golfo Nuevo (New Bay according to Fity Roy) and that it offered a good place to anchor ships.

At the time, Argentina was eager to receive immigrants, and the Argentine consul in Liverpool was keen to encourage migration and started securing land titles in Patagonia.

Reverend Jones knew that most of those interested in emigrating were not wealthy people and, at his own expense, he decided to encourage this colonizing effort. A group of enthusiasts traveled around Britain giving speeches to motivate people to join this movement to emigrate to Patagonia. It sounds easy, but it is really difficult to find people willing to set up their homes, prepare to make a two-month voyage on a ship at sea, and colonize a new country about which little is known and whose only means of communication was the sea.

The fortune of Reverend Jones' wife enabled the expenses of these emigration trips to be covered. But above all it enabled them to get a ship that could make the journey to Puerto Madryn: the "Mimosa".

The cost of the trip was £12 for adults and £6 for children between the ages of 2 and 12. Unfortunately, many of them were unable to pay for the trip and signed an IOU that they would pay back with the fruits of their labour once they were settled in Patagonia.

With all their possessions on the Mimosa, including beds, 153 hopeful Welsh souls set sail for Patagonia.

The early years (1865-1866)

The landing at New Bay (Golfo Nuevo) took place on July 28th, 1865, a day that will be commemorated to this day as a public holiday for the Province of Chubut. Golfo Nuevo will be renamed "Puerto Madryn" after a place in Wales.

Lewis Jones was the delegate who helped organize the arrival of the contingent and was already in Argentina waiting for the group. While there was a lot of hope in the group, there were also doubts on arrival: the lack of drinking water worried the people.

Lewis Jones had managed to erect some precarious houses and to receive animals from the Argentine government, but given the initial dissatisfaction shown by the group, he decided to move the settlement to the Chubut River valley where they founded a fort which they named Rawson in honor of the Argentine consul who promoted the immigration in Wales.

The land was divided there in the presence of Argentine authorities and the Argentine and Welsh flags were raised. Each family received approximately 50 hectares.

The situation was not very promising: there were few farmers in the group who knew how to work the land, but the patagonian steppe was very different from the plains of Wales.

Economically the colony fared poorly in the early years, as the immigrants did not know how to cultivate the land and raise livestock, as they were mostly miners.

The first houses here were washed away by a flood in 1865, and new houses were built. The floods also washed away potato and maize crops. Rainfall in the area was much lower than the settlers had expected. That first year the harvest was a complete failure, and the Welsh colony depended on aid from the Argentine government to subsist.

Welsh families by 1900.
Unknown author, Public domain via Wikimedia Commons

The relationship with the Tehuelches

According to the chronicles of the Welsh, there was concern about an encounter with the native Tehuelches. But from the time of their arrival, and until several months later, they saw none, almost believing that there were none in Patagonia.

The first encounter was with a small group, and while there was initial mistrust on both sides, after several months of living together they found that they were harmless.

The Tehuelches were already accustomed to trade and spoke a few words of Spanish, although for the Welsh this was also a strange language. The deal was very favorable for the colony, as the lack of food was a matter of concern: in exchange for bread they received meat, as the natives were very good hunters. The Welsh received useful instructions on how to hunt wild animals such as the guanaco and, thanks to this, many of the colony's young men quickly became skilled hunters.

As the economic situation was not good in the early years, barter was the most important form of trade: not only between the Welsh but also between the Welsh and the Tehuelche: the colonists bought guanaco meat, choique, hides, feathers in exchange for bread, cloth, tobacco, flour and yerba mate, a traditional infusion of Argentina and a large part of South America.

The colony was isolated, but thanks to this beneficial relationship it was able to emerge from this bad time by learning a great deal from those who lived in this harsh environment.

Irrigation canals circa 1902.
Source: Archivo General de la Nacion Argentina.

The expansion of the Welsh Colony (1870-1889)

Part of the colony decided to move to central Argentina, in the province of Santa Fe, where the land is naturally more fertile. Another part decided to stay in Patagonia, where they discovered that the land around the Chubut River was only fertile if it was irrigated. It was there that the idea of an irrigation system by diverting the river itself was born: this small discovery marked the colony's great future.

Anyway, the harvests improved year by year as the settlers got to know the terrain and the climate better. They began to receive visitors who were surprised by the progress of this colony in such an isolated region. They started to import machinery to work the land and flour mills that characterized the Welsh colony.

Years later, almost 100 more people arrived and, little by little, a second settlement was founded on the banks of the Chubut River, called Gaiman. The colony was also served by a schooner that facilitated the sea connection with Buenos Aires.

The remarkable improvements in wheat crops and livestock work in the region motivated the former delegate of the Welsh Colony to promote a project for the construction of a railway connecting the productive area of the Chubut River with Puerto Madryn. Funds were raised in Great Britain for this event, and almost 500 new Welsh settlers are accompanying this moment of growth. Trelew is the present name of the settlement that was connected to the port in honor of Lewis Jones, who carried out this project.

The settlers also began to make way to the Andes, as the best land for cultivation on the Atlantic coast was already occupied. And so began a series of expeditions which, with the permission of the Argentine authorities, took place by 1885. There they found a fertile valley which they called Valle Hermoso or *"beautiful valley"*, although today it is known as Colonia 16 de Octubre.

This area became the subject of a dispute between Argentina and Chile. As described in the chapter on the border issues with Chile, the decision was referred to the United Kingdom, which was a neutral power that led the arbitration of the boundary between Argentina and Chile. In 1902, despite a Chilean offer of one league of land per family, they voted to remain in Argentina in this famous plebiscite witnessed by Perito Moreno and Sir Thomas Holdich.

Thanks to the success of agriculture, the population grew and today there are two towns in the Andes: Esquel and Trevelin. By 1885, the Welsh colony had 1,600 inhabitants and was able to produce some 6,000 tons of wheat: the hardships of the early days were largely overcome.

Only surviving photograph of the plebiscite witnessed by Holdich and Moreno where the Welsh settlers voluntarily adopted Argentine citizenship.
Author Unknown - Tras las huellas de los Pioneros site, Public domain, via Wikimedia Commons.

The best wheat in the world (1889)

In 1889, the Universal Exhibition was held in Paris to celebrate the centenary of the French Revolution. This great exhibition was organized and was remembered for great public works such as the Eiffel Tower, which was to become the icon of Paris.

Argentina wanted to show itself as a power and presented one of the largest and most exuberant pavilions at the show. It was practically an eclectic building measuring 65 meters by 16 meters, with a height of 30 meters and five domes on the roof. Inside, the best products of the country were exhibited: frozen meat, marble, hides and skins, wood, iron and other minerals, wines, corn, flax and wheat. There, and before the eyes of the whole world, the wheat of Chubut - that is, the wheat of the Welsh Colony of Chubut - won the gold medal.

In 1893 and 1918 the wheat also won other first prizes at the Chicago Exposition. This served to confirm that the colonists' efforts had not been in vain.

Welsh colony harvesting around 1910.
Photo: Edward Jones, public domain, via Wikimedia Commons.

From 1914 to the present day:

In time the colony proved a remarkable success, although immigration to the area after 1914 was largely from Italy, Spain, and other countries. This meant that the Welsh gradually became a minority. Also, after 1914, there was little contact between Wales and Chubut for many years and so the use of the Welsh language has declined.

The construction of a dam on the Chubut River 120 km west of Trelew, inaugurated on 19 April 1963, eliminated the risk of flooding in the Lower Chubut Valley where, on several occasions, crops suffered serious losses.

Things began to change when a large number of people from Wales visited Patagonia in 1965 for celebrations to mark the colony's 100th anniversary. Since then, there has been a huge increase in the number of visitors from Wales. Teachers are sent to help keep the language alive, and there is some social prestige in knowing the language, even among people who are not of Welsh descent, as it is considered highly educated. There are still important cultural activities, including Welsh tea and poetry, among others.

It is very common for those traveling in this area today to visit the Welsh tea houses: there you can breathe in some of the culture of the place.

In November 1995, the Princess of Wales, Lady Di, visited the Welsh colony and went for tea in the town of Gaiman. A choir welcomed her with some Welsh songs. After her death in 1997, the tea house exhibits the utensils she used. In addition, every year, on August 31st , a bouquet of red roses is placed at the foot of a display case with her photo as a tribute.

Summary:

The story of the Welsh settlement is an exciting one: people who choose to leave their home in Wales in order to preserve their customs and language. They decide to leave something tangible, such as a home and belongings in Wales, to preserve something even more valuable but intangible: their culture and language. To this end they boarded the sailing ship Mimosa in 1865 and landed in what is now the city of Puerto Madryn, where every July 28th is still commemorated as the day of the landing or arrival.

The people who began this project knew little of working the land and suffered the difficulties of isolation, dryness of the terrain, and lack of experience. Extreme poverty marked the beginning, but going back was not in the plans; they knew that a life of servitude awaited them again in Britain.

With determination to take their destiny into their own hands, the Welsh colony in Patagonia forged ahead. It established favorable relations with the natives, with the Argentine government and finally with Wales.

It is worth mentioning that the colony was the first permanent settlement of European origin in Patagonia to have its own currency and its own laws, although over the years it would later become dependent on the Argentine authorities.

In Argentina there were several colonies and it can be seen that the organized community effort helps to quickly move forward the projects of the newcomers.

Recreation of the landing of the sailboat Mimosa at Punta Cuevas, Puerto Madryn.
Photo by Gastón Cuello, unmodified under CC BY SA 4.0 license.
Date: July 28, 2015.

One of the many branches of this company founded by José Menéndez and Mauricio Braun.
Source: Archivo General de la Nación Argentina. Public Domain.

CHAPTER 16

The dark side of Patagonia

By now, the reader can imagine how hard the adaptation process was for all the newcomers. When we talk about these people who started a new life in Patagonia, we are talking about "pioneers". Many stories portray them as people with a strong spirit and an unwavering determination to overcome any obstacle that this hostile Patagonian territory might present to them. They took it upon themselves to correct Darwin, doing their utmost to turn the arid steppe into a productive place. There were many pioneers who deserve our recognition. However, this impression we have of the pioneers should not be the only one.

There were "pioneers" who also saw how precarious the situation was and used it to their advantage. Unscrupulous individuals who took advantage of the context, the authorities and of the lack of control. Only to exploit land that was not theirs to generate economic empires that have lasted to this day. Estancias run by unscrupulous people who, in partnership with others of the same ilk and in complicity with the authorities, were responsible for writing some of the saddest pages of Patagonian history.

In this and the next chapter we will talk about other "pioneers" and the allegations that fall upon them. These following allegations were made by journalists and historians, which, although silent for many years, have not been lost in the mists of history.

Kings of Patagonia

To speak of the "dark side" of the region, we must talk about the existence of big landowners. These big landowners were pioneers, or societies of pioneers, who monopolized large amounts of land in Patagonia and Tierra del Fuego. For these pioneers, who knew their way around the political lobby, the rules were not applied as they should have been. With great skill and expensive lawyers, they were able to make exorbitant land requests in the corridors of the National Congress. And when that didn't work, they took it upon themselves to place land orders in the name of front men. The important thing was to grab land in order to fill it with sheep and produce the wool that was in demand. Wool that until 1920 was exported tax-free due to the lack of customs and border control. And so, these big landowners began to amass huge fortunes. A clear example is that of José Menendez, an Asturian who started out running a general store and today his descendants own millions of hectares in Patagonia together with the most renowned company in the region: the supermarket "La Anónima".

Menendez settled in Patagonia in 1874 when he bought a store in Punta Arenas: he had gone to collect a debt from the owner of the store, but seeing an opportunity, he ended up buying the place at a bargain price. In other words, this pioneer took advantage of a crisis with great skill. By repeating the strategy, he also managed to acquire other businesses and land.

In the stormy Strait of Magellan, shipwrecks were a profitable and clandestine activity, as some people took charge of appropriating the cargo of these ships, which brought succulent profits. Menendez was also involved in salvage of shipwrecks. He was beginning to amass a small fortune and ended having his own fleet of ships that by 1892 were crossing the Magellan Strait with an "M " painted on their funnels,

About sheep farming, Menendez entered this business after buying land from two Frenchmen in San Gregorio Bay in the Strait of Magellan where, for lack of capital to invest, they were unable to continue with the business. Taking advantage of another golden opportunity, Menendez closed the first deal to enter the Patagonian sheep economy.

Taking advantage of land auctions and his political contacts, and thanks to his great economic influence, Menéndez was acquiring land and land in Argentina and Chile together with his wife María Behety. They formed the "Sociedad Anónima Importadora y Exportadora de la Patagonia", which currently has lands all over Patagonia.

Although the law was clear and established 20,000 hectares per family, for this man, these laws did not exist. He was not the only case.

The "depopulation" of Patagonia

We have previously argued that the arrival of immigrants in Argentina, and consequently in Patagonia, was for the benefit of our country. We should not question that.

What is in question is that, with the arrival of the new settlers, the presence of the native peoples mentioned before, such as the *Tehuelches*, the *Selk'nam*, and the Yámanas, began to fade away.

The history books compliant to these big landowners, say that the reason why the presence of these vigorous peoples was reduced to a minority "was the diseases brought by the white man". There may be some truth in that, but it was by no means the main reason.

In the following subtitles I will list some incredible events that took place along with the development of sheep farming in Patagonia.

Indian massacres

The native peoples began to have commercial relations in the Patagonian cities. For example, in Punta Arenas, Menéndez, in his time as a storekeeper, traded valuable items such as furs, feathers, gold, and other products with the natives for bottles of alcohol in an exchange that was completely unfavorable to the natives. The lack of economic appreciation on the part of the natives gave the storekeepers the advantage of exchanging anything precious for a few bottles of vulgar alcohol.

Years later, Menéndez and other landowners thought that the native peoples of Patagonia and Tierra del Fuego were now a grave danger, as their sheep might be stolen or killed. Or they might, in the future, claim their share of land from their governments on the basis of their histories and traditions. These risks could deprive the landowners of their future profits. According to journalist José Maria Borrero, these landowners resolved to get rid of this risk once and for all by starting what he calls the "Indian slaughter".

There were Indian hunters who spoke proudly of their murderous past, such as Mr. Bond in Santa Cruz, and the *"Chancho Colorado"* in Tierra del Fuego.

Julius Popper (1886) on one of his raids. At his feet lies a dead Selk'nam. The photo corresponds to an album that Popper gave as a gift to Argentine President Juarez Celman. *Source: Världskulturmuseet. Public Domain.*

Mr. Bond told how he and his companions were paid one pound sterling for each "pair of Indian ears" they handed in as proof of the killing. He also said that some did not have the nerve to kill them and were content to cut off their ears just to collect the reward. But when the ranchers noticed the existence of "Indians without ears" they decided to change the conditions of these nefarious contracts.

In Tierra del Fuego, an Englishman named Mac Klenan was the founder of the Menéndez estancias. To achieve his goal, he had to exterminate the natives who occupied the land within the estancias; he massacred Selk'nam and Yámanas. Mac Klenan was an inveterate alcoholic, paunchy and red-haired, which gave him the nickname of "*Chancho Colorado*" that goes for red pig. In charge of carrying out massacres across much of Tierra del Fuego, he lured the natives to places with banquets and then massacred them in groups, as killing them one by one took too long.

These massacres took place all over Patagonia, but we have little evidence of them. The few that we do have are recounted so that they will not be lost over time.

Another very particular case was that of the kidnapping of natives: for some, the aforementioned pound sterling was not enough and they sought a higher return. So, they came up with a plan to improve their profits: they patiently stalked a family of Selk'nam, and when the time was right, they threatened them at gunpoint to get them on a ship. The boat set sail for France, and on this voyage two members of the family died and their bodies were thrown into the sea. Once in France, the remaining nine members of the family were taken to Paris: the year was 1889. At the World's Fair where the world was able to see the Eiffel Tower, they were also able to meet our aborigines, driven by the greed of some repugnant individuals.

At the exhibition, the thousands of visitors who strolled through this prestigious city heard the screams of our aborigines, who were presented as "cannibals" only to generate greater amazement and illusion among the spectators. Screams that were sure to generate terror, but were in fact desperate cries for help.

Fortunately, almost all of them were returned thanks to pressure from Argentine and Chilean diplomats in Europe.

With these allegations made by José María Borrero, it is established that there is another version of why the aboriginal populations were notably reduced. We should not ignore them, as many have amassed fortunes thanks to these horrible practices.

Yamanas taken to Europe for exhibition aboard the frigate Romanche, 1883.
Photograph: J.L. Doze and E. Payen. Payen.
Source: Archivo General de la Nacion. AGN-AGAS01-rg-2508-350180.

Recruitment preferences

With the arrival of immigrants in Patagonia, the big landowners feared the creation of population centers. These landowners were the ones who controlled the arrival of foodstuffs and who controlled their prices. They were the ones who provided work for those who came to seek a life in Patagonia, but they were also the ones who sold them the basic products for daily life.

It was very common to find advertisements saying *"Workers needed for the Estancia; useless to apply if you have a family"*. The ranchers wanted to hire single men, who would work without any worries other than having a roof over their heads, and those who got a job then depended exclusively on their employer.

Since the boss had control of the stores, the products bought by the employee were deducted from his salary at inflated prices, leaving him at the end of the month almost as poor as he started it.

When the employer did not require this single employee, he could dismiss him, as the next day there would be another one waiting to join. And the cycle would start all over again.

Land hoarding was until the middle of the 20th century the enemy of the increase of the Patagonian population. These exploiters of the land were not interested in the installation of new towns or cities, but they were interested in the moment and in making wealth while they could.

There were not many families in Patagonia for many years and the employees of the estancias were single workers. They could be evicted at any time. But if they had had families in the same place, or in a nearby village, the situation would be different: we would be talking about villages, small businesses, work cooperatives, workers' societies, and all of this beyond the reach of the influence of the big landowners. That is why they tried to control this to the last consequences, and Patagonia is still today one of the least populated places in Argentina.

A Spanish and a Chilean worker in Patagonia, 1920.
Author unknown. Photo: Public domain.

Land piracy and state fraud

National authorities were absent in the Patagonian territories where there was a Judge, a Governor, and a Police Commissioner. The eye of Buenos Aires could not see clearly what was going on as far as Tierra del Fuego, and corruption and bribery carried out by rich landowners often turned the decisions of the authorities in their favor.

The following allegations were made by a civil servant and attempts were made to silence him through bribes and kickbacks, but this attempt was unsuccessful. So they had to remove him in one way or another until they found a civil servant who was on the side of the interests of the powerful.

The first complaint is about a case of "land piracy", we are talking about smuggling, since several Estancias in Argentina, extended into Chile, where they also had productive establishments. When it was convenient, sheep were moved to Chile, and when it was convenient, back to Argentina. Smuggling was visible: thousands and thousands of sheep passed through to be sheared in Chile and returned without wool to our country in cases of clandestine export, as the land belongs to the same society on both sides of the border. The lack of inspections and strong customs laws protected the interests of greedy ranchers. The same happened with the slaughterhouses, where robust animals were sent to one side of the border or the other, while skinny animals were sent back to be fed. Thanks to this denunciation, the Treasury woke up and began to carry out the necessary audits; eventually the Customs Office was established in 1920 in the Strait of Magellan. But until then, these establishments would continue to avoid paying taxes in order to fatten their wallets.

In a second allegation of another case of "land piracy", an English sheep farming company did everything possible to legally take control of an estancia after the death of a rancher with no descendants. Donald Munro, a British immigrant, had died leaving a large inheritance: an Estancia with buildings and facilities covering almost 100,000 hectares and a large number of sheep. An English company falsified documents to say that it had bought the estate from Donald Munro's heirs. The curious thing is that the heirs never existed. But this company continued to try to get its hands on the loot and tried to prove that Mr. Munro was part of their company and therefore a shareholder in it, so that on his death the company could take over the deceased's assets. But this fraudulent move also failed. The usurpers then proceeded to bribe authorities, forge signatures and were able, after great but fraudulent efforts, to obtain possession of Mr. Munro's estate. The "San Julian Sheep Farming Company" would exploit the new land for almost 20 years, until justice was awakened by an honest civil servant who declared Donald Munro's had no real heirs and succeeded in seizing these assets from the usurpers to be returned to the Argentine Treasury.

A turbulent climate

In this chapter we have transmitted some of the allegations of the journalist José María Borrero, who published the book "La Patagonia Trágica" in 1928. The allegations are serious, worrying, and tinge with darkness a history that is supposed to have been written by characters that legend places on a pedestal for being the "pioneers" of a late and postponed region such as Patagonia.

The denunciations described above were followed by silence over the years in Patagonia, far from the reach of the national authorities. The lack of control, the lack of justice, and the normalization of bribery ended up benefiting the already rich Patagonian landowners. The big landowners did everything they could to minimize expenses and maximize their income. If they did all these atrocities in broad daylight, can you imagine what they could have done behind closed doors?

In the next chapter we will talk about what these events provoked in the patagonian working class. Over the years, they have suffered many abuses, and these abuses, which were exacerbated by a lack of ethics and scruples, ended up triggering the Patagonian strikes of 1920 and 1921, events known as "Patagonia Rebelde" or *Rebellion in Patagonia.*

March of rural workers in Puerto Santa Cruz.
May 1st, 1921.
Source : Archivo General de la Nación Argentina. Inventario 34080.

CHAPTER 17

Rebellion in Patagonia
(1919-1922)

Life in Patagonia was by nature not easy.

But if we also take into account what was described in the previous chapter, we can imagine that the contexts in which a newcomer had to move in order to get an honest job in this desolate region were not the most propitious. We are talking about large Estancias, which covered almost everything that the eye could see, and landowners who could only see the wealth that these domains could provide. For this reason and in the absence of fair controls for the reasons mentioned above, the big landowners exercised a harsh control over the work market for a long time.

The immigrants arriving from Europe, although they arrived without work, brought with them syndicalist ideas, and workers' unions began to form to look after the workers and demand fair wages and fair working conditions. Influenced by what had happened in Russia in the years leading up to the revolution, anarchist ideas also arrived in the country and were very influential in Patagonia.

It was intolerable by 1910 that a large landowner could monopolize so much land and business: for example, Menéndez and his associates already owned most of Tierra del Fuego, and in Santa Cruz they ran sheep farming, industry, commerce, and shipping. Nothing was out of their hands and they had no competition. The dominance of Menéndez, the creator of "La Anónima", was absolute.

He and other big landowners were the subject of accusations such as those we reviewed in the previous chapter. Nothing has been able to tarnish the good name of these "brave pioneers" to this day.

The strike in Puerto Bories in 1919 (Chile)

The large meat packing plants that were set up in Patagonia in the early years of the 20th century were the origin of the formation of a stable working class, since in these establishments there were no seasons as there were in the Estancias. The employees would have a fixed place of work and would not take long to organize themselves into the workers' union, in accordance with the ideas coming from Europe.

The case of Puerto Bories, very close to Punta Arenas, was the first major conflict of this type, where the immigrants who worked there were subjected to cruel working conditions. One of the points of conflict was the rise in commodity prices, which were controlled by the same employers of the meat packing plant (i.e. big landowners), creating a dilemma for the employees who had to choose between eating or fighting for their ideals. Everyone knew the luxuries in which the big landowners lived, so this kind of disrespect and lack of consideration did not go down well at all. The workers' union had, in Punta Arenas, almost 6,000 members and, finally, a general strike was called which left the Punta Arenas area immobilized.

Strikers in Puerto Bories in the vicinity of Puerto Natales (1919)
Source: La Izquierda Diario.

The owners, who had a lot of influence in the lobbies, put pressure on the Chilean government in this case to take the necessary measures. This resulted in armed clashes between security forces and strikers which only led to bloodshed. The premises belonging to the workers' society were also set on fire. Unfortunately, no one was ever convicted for the massacres, as any kind of investigation never came to any conclusion.

It can only be added that the local security forces quickly intervened in favor of the businessmen and big landowners, as they are the ones who provide accommodation, clothes and food. Security and justice worked for these "kings of Patagonia" in a partial and swift manner, because of their great influence on daily life. The police stations depended more on the Estancias than on the national authorities.

This first case of rebellion and strike in Chilean Patagonia went unpunished and silenced, but it opened the door to the events that took place in Argentine Patagonia between 1921 and 1922, more precisely in the province of Santa Cruz.

The Patagonian strikes in Santa Cruz, Argentina (1921-1922)

After the First World War, the distant Patagonian territory was plunged into a crisis, mainly because of the fall in the price of wool. The British market was glutted. Even Australia and New Zealand had been unable to trade with the UK despite their even closer ties than the Patagonian region. Gone were the years between 1914 and 1918 when the demand for wool made the region a powerhouse.

Such is the fate of any territory that exploits a single product: when the price of wool rises, there is prosperity in Patagonia; but when it falls, as has been the case since 1919, unemployment, misery, repression and lower wages begin. This leads to a crisis which discourages regional trade and is a great problem for the big landowners.

In Santa Cruz, working conditions on the estancias were appalling and all this was documented by José María Borrero and also by Osvaldo Bayer in his book *"La Patagonia Rebelde"*.

On the larger estancias, there were trained personnel for specialized tasks such as mechanics, blacksmiths, or carpenters, as well as basic personnel for field work. Employees were not allowed to leave the ranch without permission. On these cattle ranches, employees worked, ate, and slept. They worked from dawn to dusk, with non-existent work contracts, almost no days off and relatively low wages. They ate the same food day and night; they dined in the dark because the employer did not provide light for the workers. They had to pay for a packet of candles themselves and slept in cramped quarters with raw wooden crates. They had to find a mattress, or else sheepskins, which they had to buy or rent from their employers.

Wages were low and employees were often paid with vouchers to buy goods on the estancia. These were overpriced products that were necessary for work or for life itself: they had to buy from their employer candles for lighting, work clothes, a coat to sleep in, footwear, and supplies to improve the meager food provided by the employer. That is to say, with the low wages they received and all these expenses they had to incur, the employee often had no savings at all, or else he went into debt, perpetuating himself in his demeaning work to pay off what he owed to his employer.

All this was accentuated by the crisis of 1919, when the big landowners transmitted their economic pressures to the workforce, who could no longer tolerate any more outrages to their dignity as employees.

The first strike in 1920

In November 1920 the workers' union of Rio Gallegos declared a general strike with the leader Antonio Soto (Spanish) at its head. The workers' demand to the ranchers was:

- Improving comfort and hygiene conditions by reducing the number of people living together in one room by using beds and abolishing bunks;

- Provide water and hygiene items; provide them with light, heating and furniture in meeting places;

- The meal was to be varied, with soup, dessert and herbal teas;

- Provide a mattress and a first aid kit with instructions in Spanish, and undertake to return the dismissed employee to the point from which he/she was brought.

- The order also established a minimum wage and delegated clear obligations and responsibilities to the ranchers.

In front of the Sociedad Obrera (workers' union) of Río Gallego, 1920.
Source: "La Patagonia Rebelde" de Osvaldo Bayer.

The aim of this document was to vindicate the workers as human beings and to prevent them from living in miserable conditions, but rather with dignity. The minimum wage was also established, as the big meatpacking plants tended to cheat employees by signing confusing contracts whereby an employee working for a meatpacking plant in its Argentinean headquarters was paid in foreign currency, thus reducing his income considerably. The contract offered *"one hundred pesos per month"* which was supposed to be Argentine pesos, but in the end was in Chilean pesos, as the legal headquarters of the meat packing plant was in Punta Arenas and the salary to be received was then four times less than the income expected by the employee.

It is inexplicable that in the 20th century such denunciations and outrages could exist. The ranchers rejected this request and the strike spread throughout Patagonia. The strikers tried to use boycotts and strikes as their main weapons.

In February 1921, the Argentine army arrived in Santa Cruz under the command of Lieutenant Varela, who, at the request of the governor of the territory, sought to pacify the situation without resorting to arms. So, Lieutenant Varela made a tour of the estancias in the province where he acknowledged the demands of the strikers and asked them to abandon their attitude in order to finally reach an agreement. The conflict reached the beginning of a solution through an arbitration by the governor of Santa Cruz, which was accepted by the parties and approved by the National Department of Labor.

After the agreement with the governor, Varela's troops returned to Buenos Aires. But immediately after their departure, the *estancieros* (ranchers) began to break the agreement and to take reprisals against the main strikers.

The *Sociedad Rural* (association of powerful landowners) began to exert its influence in Buenos Aires, and launched a campaign in the national to denounce the anarchist danger, and slander the unprotected workers who were trying to make themselves heard as best they could. This led the workers' union from Río Gallegos led by Antonio Soto to weaken and lose credibility with the territory's authorities.

The second strike in 1921

On October of the same year, the premises of the workers' wnion in Río Gallegos, Puerto Deseado, San Julián, Puerto Santa Cruz were raided and closed down, and the leaders were arrested. The General Secretary of the union, was arrested and tortured by the police. He was later deported together with other leaders. In the light of these events, a general strike was again declared in Santa Cruz.

Antonio Soto, who was in the *Cañadón León* area (actual Gobernador Gregores City), began to promote the strike and the seizure of estancias. The police, influenced by the ranchers, began a hasty offensive and arrested the leaders whom Soto sent to Río Gallegos. They were tortured and deported. The wave of arrests of leaders in the coastal towns isolated the strike movement, which continued to grow.

Rural workers detained at Estancia Anita (1921)
Author unknown.

A parallel group of strikers calling itself "El Consejo Rojo" (The Red Council) was more aggressive than Antonio Soto, who did not want to confront the army and the government. This radical group occupied ranches, kidnapped ranchers, and carried out destruction. Soto did not agree with these practices and promised to make amends to the victims. Everything went from bad to worse in the province of Santa Cruz, which was embroiled in armed clashes between lawlessness and order.

At this point, the president of the Argentine nation, Hipólito Yrigoyen, decided to send Lieutenant Varela back again to pacify the region. Varela had made a good impression on the strikers as he had confirmed their claims for the improvements demanded in the new agreement.

Repression and bloodshed in Santa Cruz

Lieutenant Varela returned to Santa Cruz in November 1921 with orders to end the strike. And now, under the influence of the big landowners, Varela took the decision to apply death penalty to all the strikers.

Army mobilizing in Santa Cruz (1921)
Author unknown.

Accompanied by 200 well-armed soldiers, he began to repress the different columns of strikers. Some of them were tricked into coming to negotiate, but they were ambushed and killed in cold blood, as was the case of José Font, a workers' union leader who had joined Antonio Soto.

In other clashes, the Argentine military overpowered the strikers by shooting them by the dozens without a fair trial. Blood was spilled mercilessly all over the province, causing astonishment among the same ranchers who, at first, agreed with the measures taken by Lieutenant Varela.

In Osvaldo Bayer's books, there are anecdotes of when the workers were arrested and before being shot, the ranchers begged for mercy for some of them who were the most skilled, such as mechanics, blacksmiths, carpenters, among others. Some were able to escape these atrocities.

As a result of the bloody decision taken by Lieutenant Varela, the last strikers decide to take refuge at Estancia Anita, between El Calafate and the Perito Moreno Glacier. There they discussed at length whether to surrender or flee: Antonio Soto urged them to flee, saying that if they surrendered they would be shot, despite the promises of the Argentine army, which sought to capture Soto as the leader of the revolt. A large part of the last strikers decided to surrender, while Soto escaped from the place by crossing the border into Chile, where he took refuge under another name.

The decision of the assembly at Estancia Anita put an end to the strike movement. With Soto gone, the *Sociedad Obrera* (the workers Union) ceased to exist.

The surrendered strikers were tortured for a whole night, forced to hold a candle and prevent it from going out. The next day they were forced to dig their own graves and were shot *on the spot.*

In all, an estimated fifteen hundred workers were shot during Lieutenant Varela's second visit to Patagonia. This fact meant the end of the workers' demands, the end of the Workers' Society, and the silencing of all allegations against the estancia owners, for at least 50 years, until the books written by the historian Osvaldo Bayer in the work known as "La Patagonia Rebelde" came to light. For this book he interviewed many characters from both sides who were still alive in the 1970s and was able to reconstruct with justice the dark events described in this and the previous chapter. I recommend his reading for those who wish to dig deeper into this chapter of Patagonian history.

Summary of the Patagonian strikes

The aims of the strikes were to vindicate the workers and to improve their living and working conditions, which, as was exposed, were deplorable: living and working cost them their wages and then they closed their work cycle poorer than they had entered their jobs. Without electricity, without adequate housing, and without a living wage, they had to resign themselves to surviving without a family in Patagonia.

The lack of fair control by insufficient authorities and the distance to Buenos Aires meant that the versions of the strike were distorted by the powerful ranchers who published paid articles in the national press, soiling the already weak organized workers.

Although Lieutenant Varela at the first opportunity tried to pacify the region, giving the strikers' arguments as valid and bringing both sides to an agreement, this failed when the lieutenant left Patagonia. The situation quickly became tense, and illegal repression by the police influenced by the estancia owners led to armed clashes returning with greater force. TVarela had to return, sent by a president who was under a lot of pressure. In Santa Cruz he was approached by the ranchers, who also presented an aggravated version, and without listening to the strikers, he adopted a severe position: shooting the strikers.

The strikers, armed and motorized, had to face the Argentine army to save their lives and protect their ideals. (1921).
Author unknown.

These facts make up another dark chapter of our Patagonia: another genocide.

Rural workers detained at Estancia Anita, they were forced to hold a candle overnight and death penalty was applied next day. They were buried in the surroundings of the Estancia. (1921).
Author unknown.

The first Argentine genocide was that of the native peoples during the "Conquest of the Desert": on that occasion these peoples were transformed into the enemies of progress, branded as uneducated and barbaric so that public opinion would approve of this "war" against the Indians.

This second genocide was now against "civilized beings" who were only fighting for their rights and ideals. But they were unheard and punished for standing up against the progress of a few.

Complaints were hushed up. Pseudo-slavery was maintained on many Patagonian estancias for fear of reprisals. And the same few individuals continued to amass fortunes at the expense of the hard work of many.

Today, on the road in front of Estancia Anita, near El Calafate, stands a monument that reads *"Memory, Truth, and Justice"* for the workers massacred in this place and in representation of all the fallen. One hundred years after these bloody events, those who supported the strike out of well-founded and documented conviction are beginning to be vindicated.

Estancia Anita, owned by the Menendez-Behety company, is closed to the public.

For those who wish to know more about these tragic events, I recommend reading the works of Borrero ("la Patagonia trágica"), Bayer ("la Patagonia rebelde" - there is also a film with a screenplay by Bayer himself) and Alonso Marchante ("Menendez, Rey de la Patagonia").

Lake Gutierrez near Bariloche (1915)
Author: Alberto M. de Agostini

CHAPTER 18

The creation of National Parks (1903)

Long-term thinking is not a gift that abounds in Argentina. Much less is it imaginable that more than 100 years ago someone would have thought of planting such a valuable and exemplary seed as the creation of a National Park in Argentina. Before then, the environmental degradation, the continuous retreat of the natural environment, the extinction of animal and plant species, and the disfigurement of landscapes were already well known. For this reason, conservation-minded people from all over the world have sought, since the second half of the 19th century, the creation of nature reserves to ensure the survival of the most spectacular areas as well as the most interesting biological communities.

In Argentina, that person was called Francisco Pascasio Moreno. Yes, the same one we talked about earlier: for decades he devoted himself to researching the Patagonian mountain range and his knowledge of the area led him to be one of the experts who worked for 22 years on the delimitation of the border between Chile and Argentina.

The origin of the current system of protected natural areas dates back to the year 1903, when on November 6th, Dr. Francisco Pascasio Moreno - an outstanding Argentine explorer, geographer and paleontologist - in a note addressed to the then Minister of Agriculture, expressed his wish to donate to the country a piece of land in the vicinity of Bariloche with the express purpose of maintaining its natural physiognomy and that the works to be carried out would only be those that would facilitate the comfort of the visitor's life. His wish was that this natural reserve would be for the enjoyment of present and future generations.

This significant donation arose from the cession of land in his favor by President Julio Roca as an extraordinary reward for the free services rendered to the country during 22 years. The donation of this fraction of land was made with the exclusive condition of being reserved as a "*National Park without any concession to private indi-*

viduals", it was accepted by Decree of the National Executive Power on February 1st 1904, during the presidency of General Julio A. Roca, constituting the nucleus of the current Nahuel Huapi National Park. For Moreno, this area possessed the most interesting gathering of natural beauties he had observed in Patagonia.

With the government's acceptance of this legacy, Argentina became the third country in the Americas, and the fifth in the world, with national parks, along with the United States, Australia, Canada and New Zealand.

Man before Lake Nahuel Huapi (1917)
Photo: Frank y Frances Carpenter Collection.
Source: Library of Congress Prints and Photographs Division Washington, D.C. 20540 USA

The early years of the National Parks of Argentina

This decision of Moreno was for this to be the seed of the other National Parks that were to follow.

In 1908, Argentine President José Figueroa Alcorta would add another 43,000 hectares to the Nahuel Huapi National Park. Some 75,000 hectares had also been set aside in northeastern Argentina on the border with Brazil, in what is now Iguassu Falls, but the lack of infrastructure and personnel was still noticeable.

At the beginning of this institution, the central power had a strong political interest in reaffirming Argentine sovereignty in the confines of Patagonia. This was also the case of Iguassu, in order to strengthen its presence in areas bordering Brazil in the northeast. The institution's aim was to make more effective the possession of regions considered marginal at the time.

After his gesture of solidarity, Moreno continued as director of the Museum of La Plata. He worked as a national deputy, was founder of the Boy Scouts, among so many activities, generally unpaid and which led him into debt. In 1919, almost without fortune, Francisco Moreno died in the city of Buenos Aires and was buried in the Recoleta Cemetery (Buenos Aires) next to his wife, María Ana Varela. In 1920, the National Bank of Argentina judicially auctioned off all his assets to cover his debts and outstanding credits without even showing any kind of consideration for a person who gave his life and work to the future of our nation.

In that way, Perito Moreno said farewell to this world, without being able to see the seed he sowed in 1903 fully blossom.

Homage to the Perito Francisco Pascasio Moreno
one hundred years after his death.
Representatives of National Parks and the Scout community salute him. These institutions
were created by him.
Source: argentina.gob.ar

The new National Parks Administration (1934)

In 1934, the legal basis for the creation of national protected areas was sanctio-
ned. This law created the General Administration of National Parks and Tourism.
This new institution, which was intended to have much more influence over the
towns or areas where they were erected, was led by Exequiel Bustillo, who with his
team of collaborators, developed a vast foundational work with roads, paths, inns,
park rangers' houses, and hotels. A civilizing work was achieved by constructing
public buildings: schools, churches, hospitals, railway stations, etc, in the towns of
Iguassu, Angostura, San Martín de los Andes, and Bariloche, of which the current
building of the Civic Center, which can be visited even today in the center of this
city, is a good example.

With a view to continuing the policy initiated after the enactment of the aforementioned law, in September 1936 the Executive submitted to Congress a bill proposing the creation of new protected areas, and by decree of 11 May 1937, the Lanín, Los Alerces, Perito Moreno and Los Glaciares National Parks were created, all of them located in Patagonia. The decree also provided for an area annexed to Los Alerces, which only in 1971 would constitute the Lago Puelo National Park. Already with a visible improvement and a remarkable structural development, Argentina's National Parks boasted of being the guardians of the most beautiful areas of our country, becoming a magnet for visitors from all over the world.

In 1944, the descendants of Francisco Pascasio Moreno decided to transfer his remains to Bariloche, where they were emotionally laid to rest. His coffin was covered with the Argentine flag and three ponchos that belonged to the Tehuelche chiefs Saihueque, Pincén, and Catriel; symbolizing the integration of the Argentine Nation with the aboriginal peoples. Moreno's coffin was then transferred to Centinela Island in the ship "Modesta Victoria", whose name is now carried by another ship that also sails the Nahuel Huapi.

National Park and lake Nahuel Huapi.
Source: Archivo General de la Nacion.

Conflicts within Patagonia's National Parks

When almost all the national parks in southern Argentina were created, there were already some human settlements in the areas they encompassed. These establishments exploited the land commercially with livestock or by exploiting the local timber. Several Estancias were located within the territories delimited by the National Parks.

With the leasing contracts we explained before, a number of pioneers settled in most of the fertile valleys in the hope that these lands would be granted to them, eventually in ownership, by the state. This possibility vanished with their incorporation into the national parks system, as the exploitation of the land runs completely counter to the objectives of protected areas.

In any case, the National Parks Administration admitted these settlers, restricting their activity to some extent, establishing a maximum number of livestock and prohibiting the felling of trees and hunting. These permits are non-transferable, which made it possible to end the economic exploitation upon the death of the owners, with the consequent recovery of the land for the conservation of nature.

The conflicts brought about by the presence of rural establishments are various:

It is important to note that overgrazing leads to erosion. That way, the focus on nature protection is lost. Given the nature of the terrain, it is very difficult to exercise effective controls and the number of livestock often exceeds the permitted number.

Estancias or its staff poaching, or the harassment of wildlife by its dogs, was a major problem. The persecution of species potentially harmful to sheep or cattle (such as pumas and foxes) ignoring the priority that wildlife preservation should take over other interests in these areas is an example to be taken into account.

The overexploitation of timber, either for consumption or sale, causes clearings in the forests and, finally, the fires caused by carelessness of these people who roam freely throughout the area and in all seasons.

However, on the other hand, several of these settlers have accepted to reconvert their activities, discarding agricultural activities and replacing them with the provision of visitor support services (camping sites, accommodation, horse rental, etc.) fully in line with the management objectives of the protected areas in which they are inserted.

Reconversion of an Estancia

In Patagonia, the example of finding even Estancias that predate the creation of national parks is a common one. In my professional career I have had the good fortune to work for Estancia Cristina, which is today a tourist enterprise that offers full-day excursions, as well as the opportunity to stay in a high-class hotel. Estancia Cristina had been founded in 1914 before the creation of the Glacier National Park in 1937 and its owners, originally from England, could not own the land they worked. In 1937 they received this occupancy permit issued by the National Parks Administration.

This permit allowed them to work the land with some restrictions in order to protect the sustainability of the National Park's ecosystem. The permit was non-transferable and can only be transferred to the direct descendants of this family, in this case, the Masters family.

Although the Estancia was focused in sheep farming, from the 1950s onwards mountaineers and tourists who had heard about this beautiful place began to arrive here. Little by little this Estancia was transformed from a sheep-farming business to a tourism business.

In 1997, with a rich history behind it, the Masters family died out after the passing of its last member. Estancia Cristina came under the exclusive jurisdiction of Los Glaciares National Park.

In 1999, a private company took over the concession of Estancia Cristina with the aim of exploiting the place for tourism and taking on the role of guardian of this isolated corner of Los Glaciares National Park.

Today Estancia Cristina receives tourists from October to April every year, where they discover not only the beauties of the National Park, but also the wonderful history of a family of pioneers who chose that corner to make a life for themselves in Patagonia.

Estancia Cristina is home to a museum, of which I am proud to be the curator. This research led to the project of writing the book you are reading right now.

Estancia Cristina, inside National Park Los Glaciares.
Photograph kindly shared by Juan Pablo Raposo.

Argentina's National Parks today

There are currently a couple of new National Parks in the process of being created, but we are talking about approximately 35 such enclosures for the protection of different ecosystems.

The National Parks manage their own resources, and have the capacity to decide how to distribute them in order to effectively fulfill their conservation tasks. For those of us who love nature it seems to be one of the most sacred entities we can find, but often the reality can be different: these entities are sometimes run by people whose scruples are few and far between and give rise to strange occurrences.

Currently, in Los Glaciares National Park, the fate of the Perito Moreno glacier is tied to the Santa Cruz River, which stretches from Lago Argentino to the Atlantic Ocean. On this historic river, crossed by Darwin, Fitz Roy, and the Perito Moreno, a pair of mega-dams under construction could flood more than 500 km² of the region, an area almost twice as large as Buenos Aires. This catastrophe could transform the vast, millennia-old glacial river that flows freely between the Patagonian Ice Field and the Atlantic Ocean.

The national government has insisted that the current dam project will not damage the Perito Moreno Glacier, a natural jewel of our country.

Argentina's National Parks Administration showed a weak, unclear posture on this matter. This provoked the fury of many of its employees, and in turn of the local residents of El Calafate (directly linked to Los Glaciares National Park, its dependence on tourism and its commitment to the environment). A group of activists from the Province of Santa Cruz sent them a letter in 2017 complaining about the "poor position" of the institution during the public hearing on the progress of the two hydroelectric power plants that are now being built with inconclusive environmental impact studies. The disappearance of natural heritage (the Glaciers and the Southern Patagonian Ice Field), as well as cultural heritage (ancient Tehuelche settlements on the banks of the Santa Cruz River), seems not to be of vital importance to our authorities. Only time will be the judge of these actions.

In short, the National Parks of Argentina have a great challenge, which is to follow in the footsteps of their creator, the Perito Francisco Pascasio Moreno: a character who put aside his personal economic wealth to give us all a natural heritage that today, in some cases, has also been declared a World Heritage Site by UNESCO. Those of us who once worked in relation to this institution hope that the course set by Moreno can be recovered.

Aerial cage crossing the Neuquén River, at the height of Chos Malal, 1915.
Argentine Patagonia.
Archivo General de la Nación Argentina
Documento fotográfico. Inventario 77806

CHAPTER 19

Communication and logistics in Patagonia

Overcoming distance and loneliness was one of the most constant challenges for the men and women who struggled to adapt to such a hostile and remote environment as Patagonia.

Many of these early settlers perished because of the isolation of living in such a place in the hope of building a better future for themselves.

Others relied on news that came in dribs and drabs from the Old World, some by ship, some by telegraph, and even by radio. Many received monthly subscriptions to magazines that served as a hobby, or even to learn about the latest technological advances. Little by little, Patagonia became connected to the rest of the world; and consequently, connected to each other to gradually improve the quality of life of its long-suffering inhabitants.

In this chapter we will discuss communication developments over the years in Patagonia, Argentina.

Correo Argentino: the Argentine Postal Service

Argentina inherited from colonial times a mail service that, although it was in line with the advances of the time, lacked the necessary deployment to communicate with its population. Progress began in Buenos Aires, where the head office was located and which gradually opened branches throughout the country. As a state institution, the Post sought to offer low prices in order to encourage the use of the service and to give citizens the feeling that communication between two points in the country was within reach.

In 1876, the first great step was taken when the Post merged with the Telegraph service, in order to provide a complete and appropriate service to the citizens. At the same time, internally, the Post began to structure itself in such a way that it managed to sanction an internal regulation that even included uniforms for each of its functions. At that time, there were already 3,700 employees working to communicate the whole country. The Post already had a development that began to be sustained over time, trying to resemble the Central European postal service.

The Post not only carried mail and telegraphic correspondence, but also began to provide other services, such as money orders. But as the Post was present throughout the Argentine territory, it could not avoid the duty of annexing tasks that were not always related to its specific function.

It was like an auxiliary for other entities that were created and needed support in the national territory: it had to participate in the National Census and in the Elections, just to name a few. The Post had to do this over the years with the help of its employees who, with almost little training, but with a lot of flexibility, took on these responsibilities with a lot of obedience, proudly representing this institution.

As we said: with low tariffs, revenues were not enough to cover the costs of such a structure scattered all over the country. Contrary to the rest of the world's postal services which sought to balance income and expenditure, the main objective in Argentina was to communicate and connect the country, despite the fact that here it was a loss-making entity.

Dos Pozos Post Office (southern Chubut) ca. 1899.
Unknown author - Archivo familiar presente en el Archivo de Recuerdos del Valle Inferior del Rio Chubut, Public Domain via Wikimedia Commons.

The telegraph in Patagonia

Patagonia was to be almost entirely connected by 1902 through telegraph lines. A main line ran along the Atlantic coast, while a second line extended into the Andes range and then back to meet the coastline. This was made possible by thousands of kilometers of iron wires hanging from palm trees that came from the forests of Paraguay and were installed in these Patagonian corners.

The materials also included lapacho wood crossarms and Argentine porcelain insulators, all of which were transported by sea from north to south. The materials withstood the climatic conditions of the region very well, but they were also assisted by Post Office personnel.

As the line progressed, offices were set up to monitor the status of the telegraph line. These precarious offices were set up every hundred and fifty kilometers, and provided mail service to the few inhabitants of the area of influence. There were two people living in these offices: one served the customers, while the other traveled the line to supervise and repair it if necessary. The major problems on the telegraph line were due to the strong winds in the region. The most common damage was the cutting of the wires or the breaking of the palm trees.

The telegraph service grew along with the population of Patagonia, and its pioneers who, having settled in such an isolated place, began to receive small drops of progress in our country.

Mail by sea and then by land:

Maritime mail was fundamental for Patagonia, as we have seen so far in our book: The sea was the connection with the rest of the world. But over the years, and along with the officialization of a mail service, national transports and private companies came to be used to carry mail and passengers. Ships carried mail until 1945, when they were completely replaced by land mail, with the exception of Tierra del Fuego, which continued to receive sea mail.

From these ports on the Atlantic coast, roads began to head west towards the Andes Mountains. With these roads, Correo Argentino began to fulfill its functions by land and also by setting up offices in the interior of Patagonia. The first vehicles arrived in Patagonia in 1910, replacing the horse, inaugurating the era of motorized mail in the region.

Mule-drawn carts in Neuquen, Patagonia Argentina. (1920)
Source: Archivo General de la Nación.

The mail drivers had to drive on precarious, rock-strewn roads, kicking up a cloud of dust in the windy summers, or else plowing through swamps and battling snow and frost in winter. An adventure in the best "Rally" style. There are many, many stories of these motorized couriers as they connect to Patagonia, and these characters get into the hearts of the people. In this chapter I am pleased to tell you the story of a Patagonian means of transport from the middle of the 20th century known as "El Cordillerano".

"El Cordillerano": Freight and passenger ground transport

I had the pleasure of meeting Marcelo "*Titi*" Schupbach, who at almost 90 years of age told me his anecdotes about driving this transport.

El Cordillerano was a transport company that made a weekly trip from Puerto San Julián on the coast of Santa Cruz Province to Lago Pueyrredón in the Andes Mountains.

It departed on Saturdays from Puerto San Julián, making several stops in different towns, where the Hotel was usually the meeting point. There, the drivers would stop to rest, eat something, or spend the night if necessary. At that time, at the side of the road there were mailboxes belonging to different estancias, where the mail was deposited and then picked up by the staff of each estancia.

One of the vehicles was a Ford and the other an REO Speedwago carrying between 14 and 21 passengers: the mail was either on the roof or inside the vehicle. As these buses had a front engine, heating consisted of the exhaust pipe running under the passenger seats and radiating heat into the vehicle.

It also transported the wounded and sick to hospitals, and fulfilled functions that it should not have, as it was a vital service for the communication of such isolated parts of Patagonia.

What "Titi", remembered most was the wind they had to fight against, because the vehicles went at 60 or 70 kilometers per hour at the most, and sometimes the wind beat them by a wide margin. Sometimes passengers had to push the bus up hills, and also the bus had to cross the Furioso River to reach its final destination where there were no bridges yet.

It was the first transport that linked the sea with the mountain range and carried out all kinds of orders such as medicines, messages, salaries, correspondence, transport of the sick and wounded, and was a big part of Patagonian life.

It traveled some 650 kilometers each way and carried messages, hopes, and loved ones of Patagonian life.

Today, one of the buses is in the Perito Moreno National Park, one of its old stops in the province of Santa Cruz, after many years of service to the Patagonian people. In actual Estancia La Oriental, the bus rest spending its retirement greeting its visitors.

El "Cordillerano" driving also in winter.
Courtesy Laura Devoto.

The Little Prince in Patagonia: Airmail Service

In 1929, the pilot and writer Antoine de Saint-Exupéry arrived in Argentina. He had been asked to come to our country to help the *Aeroposta Argentina* company to open and exploit new routes dedicated to air mail transport. His task was to start up the Patagonian air routes so that the *Correo Argentino* would have the chance to improve its connections to such distant lands.

In November 1929, the route between Bahía Blanca (south of Buenos Aires) and Comodoro Rivadavia (a coastal city in Patagonia that grew thanks to the discovery of oil) was opened. With this inauguration the inhabitants could be better connected and put an end to regional isolation. Initially, there were be two flights a week between these cities.

In March 1930, Saint-Exupéry inaugurated flights to Río Gallegos. After a long study of the route, he managed to land in the capital of Santa Cruz, welcomed by the authorities and a joyful crowd. Argentine Patagonia felt as never before that it was definitely integrated with the rest of the country.

On the left, with beret: Rufino Luro Cambaceres, Argentine aviator.
In the middle: Julio Aloyz.
On the right, with goggles: Antoine de Saint-Exupéry.
Date: 1929
Location: Puerto San Julián - Santa Cruz, Argentina.
Courtesy: "Mi Río Gallegos".

At that time, it was necessary to fly at night in order to gain time compared to other means of transport. This practice was very dangerous and inspired the pilot to write his book "Night Flight". Patagonia did not go unnoticed by Antoine de Saint-Exupéry. His passage as a pilot through our Patagonian sky and the direct contact with the people of this far south, remained forever in his memories, which were later captured in his literary creations.

Thanks to him and many other pilots, postal communication in Patagonia by air got off to a prosperous start.

Radio amateurs

The radio played a fundamental role in intercommunication, especially for the estancias, given their isolation throughout the Patagonian region.

Not only were there radio amateurs, but there were also local radio stations that broadcast frequencies, transmitting at set times so that workers and inhabitants of distant fields could listen to the radio at those times and receive messages. The messages become vitally important in times of rain or snowfall and also if there is an emergency.

In order to generate electricity in rural areas, in the USA in the late 1920s the Albers brothers experimented with wind-generated electricity and designed the first prototype 6 Volt generator called the *Wincharger*. In Patagonia, the lack of electrical service sparked the fame of this product that would provide ranches and radio amateurs with enough power for a 6 Volt radio transmitter.

Amateur radio in Argentina was supported in its beginnings by *Correo Argentino*, in order to be able to issue the corresponding licenses and an internationally accepted code of conduct. It was practiced as an indispensable means of communication, but also as a hobby to overcome isolation, especially in this region. For radio communication to work, one had to wait for good weather with clear skies and little wind.

Ham Radio Operator (1924)
Source: Archivo General de la Nación. Documento Fotográfico. Inventario 108133

Successful communications between radio amateurs are usually confirmed by means of postcards called "QSL". These postcards reflect in writing the details that serve to confirm the contact made with the other station; the call sign, geographic position, frequency, and mode of transmission, date and time, usually in coordinated universal time, serve as a record of the contact.

Many radio amateurs proudly display their collection of QSLs, which confirm their expertise and hard work in this hobby. It is not only the quantity that counts, but there is a real fervor in the quest to make "difficult" contacts which are rewarded with the arrival of the QSL card confirming that longed-for contact.

Difficult contacts can be, for example, finding the frequency to talk to someone in Patagonia. Working at the Estancia Cristina Museum, I made an inventory of over 2,000 QSL cards and several of them read: "please send me your card: you are my first contact in Patagonia".

Yaesu radio equipment exhibited at the Estancia Cristina Museum.
Own photo.

Communication in Patagonia today:

Patagonia did not experience significant growth of its population. What did grow were the provincial capitals, or the different industrial or tourist centers. That is to say that the roads remain the same, and the condition of these is normally acceptable. But infrastructure development in Patagonia is generally slow. There are still many gravel roads in this region.

Mail works well, although telecommunications have lots of room for improvement. In 2014 there were still two options of internet speeds to choose from at service providers in El Calafate: 1 MBPS or 2 MBPS. Mobile reception is only available in populated areas, but then it becomes a problem to find in the open. The Patagonian villager has to choose a cell-phone company whose antenna has the best reception. Sometimes, in the same town or city, the signal strength differs depending on the neighborhood you are in.

The construction of new airports, the provision of bus routes, and duty-free port zones have given the region a different air. But the winds that blow are always an impediment to the correct transmission of messages in this far-flung Patagonian region.

BOCAMINA DE RIO TURB

Coal mining in Patagonia.
Río Turbio coal mine, Santa Cruz 1944.
Source: Archivo General de la Nación Argentina.
AGN_DDF/ Caja 1055, inv. 40490.

CHAPTER 20

Agriculture and the natural resources

The Patagonian region has one of the oldest soils on Earth: it was a part of Gondwana, as we discussed in the first chapter. Now we will talk about the natural resources we can find today in the region, their relationship with the geological history of the place and also the economic impact their discovery brought.

Thanks to the hundreds of millions of years and cycles of animal and plant life that took place in the Patagonian region over time, the terrain became increasingly richer. Nor can we forget other aspects such as: the advance and retreat of the sea, the rise of the Andes Mountain Range, and the effect of glaciations on the terrain. These are processes that modeled and changed the configuration of environments, for example, by raising land that had been left deep in the Earth, exposing minerals that were produced under the Earth's crust. These processes are slow and complex.

On a more practical note, resources such as oil, natural gas and coal have been discovered and exploited in the Patagonian region throughout the 20th century.

A part of Gondwana is present-day Patagonia. On these grounds there used to be a tropical forest where the largest dinosaurs that existed on Earth lived. With the rise of the Andes Mountain Range, a period of volcanism apparently led to the extinction of these animal and plant species. New minerals covered the region and all these species, which over hundreds of millions of years, led to a process of fossilization. This process of slow decomposition in the depths of today's Patagonian steppe under extreme conditions has led to the generation of what we know today as fossil fuels.

Discovery of oil in Argentine Patagonia (1907)

Comodoro Rivadavia is a city founded in 1901, located south of the Welsh-founded settlements of Puerto Madryn and Trelew, on the Atlantic coast, in what is now the province of Chubut. Since its foundation, the settlers encountered serious problems with the supply of drinking water, as it had to be transported by carts from several kilometers.

In 1903, with the help of a drilling machine, they tried to look for water, but were unsuccessful, reaching a depth of no more than 200 meters. Perito Moreno, who at the time surveyed the region, had spoken to the engineers who were searching for water and assured them that it was easier to find oil than water in this area due to its geological characteristics. He also offered to help them find better drilling machines.

Years later, and thanks to these efforts, a new drilling machine landed in Comodoro Rivadavia and with it it was possible to reach greater depths. And so, on December 13, 1907, in a search for water, oil was discovered at a depth of 540 meters. It is said that the telegram that informed Buenos Aires of this event simply said *"Searching for water, oil was found"*.

This accidental discovery led to legal measures to protect our country's underground heritage for the first time. It also led to the uncontrolled growth of the city.

First oil well in Comodoro Rivadavia, Chubut, Argentina. Date 1907.
Source: Archivo General de la Nación. Inventario 45883.

From those early years, it was necessary to have a workforce to carry out the oil activity. The well was located three kilometers from the village. This, and the tradition in the oil industry of settling the workers near the oil wells, led the authorities to build sheds and barracks for the settlement of the workers. There was a large population growth, but also a great lack of investment. Wage and housing conditions were very precarious, which also led to protests that were answered by the navy. We remember that the influence of Russian anarchism was very strong in Patagonia. Repression and deportation were the common currency with which they tried to put down the protests during the early years.

The discovery of a new well in northern Patagonia, and international pressures for control of this resource, led Argentina to create a new public institution called YPF (Federal Oil Reserves), which responded to different economic factors that came together at the end of the First World War. Oil was a highly prized resource and its protection was prioritized. It is worth noting that this state institution was later privatized and in recent years returned to the Argentine state.

However, the discovery of oil brought new economic activity and new prospects to the region. Comodoro Rivadavia had been founded to have a port to export the region's wool, and eventually became an oil center par excellence in Patagonia.

Coal in Santa Cruz

This is attributed to the discovery of coal outcrops in the Río Turbio area (now Santa Cruz province) by an Argentinean expedition in 1887. After the discovery, there was no further progress in its exploitation until the fuel restrictions imposed by the Second World War made it necessary to diversify the energy matrix of the Argentine Republic. It is worth noting that until the middle of the 20th century, Argentina imported coal.

The history of the town of Río Turbio is linked from the beginning to the creation of another state company named YCF (Federal Coal Reserves), whose main purpose was to exploit the coal seams of which its existence was known since the time of the expedition mentioned above, but given the current global situation, Argentina sought to solve the problem by promoting self-sufficiency in coal.

Miner working in Rio Turbio, Santa Cruz. No date.
Source: Archivo General de la Nación AR-AGN-AGAS01-rg-Caja 731 – Inventario 206250

YCF was already in existence, and by 1943 it was responsible for the opening and initial operation of the so-called Mine 1 with a small number of workers in camps.

With the start of this activity, the area prospered, and in 1951 a 258-kilometer-long industrial gauge railway was inaugurated, whose tracks linked Río Turbio with Río Gallegos that was the port for shipment.

It was the arrival of the railway that gave the area a wide growth, helping to supply the population with supplies and also the necessary machinery. This railway has very particular characteristics, such as having the narrowest gauge in Patagonia. The train works strictly for the company and has only occasionally carried passengers. Punta Loyola, in Río Gallegos, is a deep-water port on the Atlantic coast.

In recent years, work began on the installation of a thermal power plant with a capacity of 240 MW, and once completed it will contribute energy to the national grid, to which it was connected for the first time in August 2015. It is the southernmost coal-fired power plant in the world and a major boost to Patagonia's economic development.

Río Turbio city has almost 10,000 inhabitants today.

Cargo train running between Rio Turbio mines and the port Rio Gallegos
Source: Archivo General de la Nacion.

Decline of sheep farming

In this book we have reviewed the history of Patagonian sheep farming, positioning the estancias as productive establishments par excellence in this region.

Unfortunately, this business also suffered the consequences of the various global events that changed the economy.

To begin with, the high demand for wool at the beginning of the 20th century was favored by the ample land Patagonia offered. At the same time, Patagonia's geostrategic location on the Strait of Magellan gave it an unbeatable export situation. And with the outbreak of the First World War, the price of wool was sky-high. A better scenario could not be envisaged.

But after the end of the First World War, the price of wool began to fall again. In 1914, the Panama Canal came into operation, gradually taking over the Strait of Magellan. And internally, rural strikes had brought the big landowners into serious difficulties.

The price of wool would continue to fall slowly, with a brief upturn during the Second World War. After this conflict, Argentina began to lose its leading role in the wool market to Australia and New Zealand, which had improved their production processes by offering high quality raw material.

Finally, sheep farming in Patagonia was so extensive that soil recovery was too slow. There are areas where we find desertification because the terrain could not support the huge number of animals that have grazed on it. Plus, the poor level of rainfall prevents the hard Patagonian pastures from growing again. This also generates a detriment of productive areas, complicating those people who still dedicate themselves to the activity.

According to official data, Argentina once had almost eighty million sheep; today we are talking about only twelve million sheep.

This can be seen in two ways: either the exploitation of wool was just an economic opportunism that was not intended for the long term, or wool is really a product that is no longer sought after by customers, who now have access to cheaper synthetic materials for clothing.

In any case, the Estancias are still there, fighting against time and the wind, which still seems to want to banish them.

An empty shearing shed.
Photo courtesy of Juan Pablo Raposo.

The wind

Within the range of alternative energies, wind power is an opportunity for Argentina. The country's winds, especially those of Patagonia, contain energy that could be captured to become part of our energy matrix, but the lack of projects has complicated the possibility of their development. According to data from the Latin American Wind Energy Association, Argentina has enormous potential, but we must not lose sight of the fact that wind energy must compete against the costs of other more conventional energy sources. The current reality is that wind energy is generally considered to be an unprofitable resource. Often the problem is that the initial investments are often compared. There is no doubt that the installation costs of a wind turbine are higher than the costs of conventional gas or oil-fired power plants. But in the long run, a conventional power plant has to invest a lot of money in fuel for its operation. Wind, on the other hand, is a free input. The operating cost of a wind power plant over its lifetime is infinitely lower than the operating cost of a thermal power plant.

Many travelers come to Patagonia, and when they see the endless landscape and feel the winds, they ask themselves the same question as those of us who live here: "Why not?".

There are some wind farms in Patagonia, yes, but it seems that our country is still focused on non-renewable energy resources, and private efforts are not enough to demonstrate the true potential of wind energy.

It will be a matter of time before we know how this story will continue.

Other natural resources

As mentioned above, the Patagonian region offers a wide spectrum of minerals and metals. Patagonia is a region where the possibilities for economic development are limited, and the mining industry appears as an opportunity for local and regional transformation.

Currently, there are more mining projects looking for gold and uranium. These projects are controversial for the environment as they are referred to as mega-mining, and in Argentina, with the media case of Barrick Gold that took place in Famatina (north west of Argentina), public opinion is not in favor of these projects.

As with the mega-dam project on the Santa Cruz River, communities are torn between the need for a stable job opportunity and the protection of the environment in which they live. This division does not help the harmony of these Patagonian peoples on whom such decisions fall.

Fishing industry on the Atlantic coast of Patagonia

This activity, if it had sufficient control and if it had sufficient investment, would be one of the most prosperous in the region and in the country.

Argentina has almost five thousand kilometers of coastline and 200 miles of Exclusive Economic Zone.

But one story that is repeated every summer in the South Atlantic, and that nobody pays enough attention to, is that of the fishing boats that cross the 200-mile limit and enter Argentina's exclusive fishing zone. They duel with the outnumbered agents of the Coast Guard, and load their holds with squid and also hake and Patagonian toothfish. They take with them profits made at the expense of a protected economic zone, from which our country cannot benefit because of the lack of effective control of these waters.

These trawlers also discard tons of marine ecosystem, from seaweed to dolphins and whales. There are so many illegal fishing vessels that airline crews flying between Ushuaia and Buenos Aires describe the night scene from the air as "marine cities". Documentaries have been made, there has been a strong outcry from environmental activists, but the news is always hushed up.

Illegal fishing vessels are not just taking our wealth; they are taking our jobs, our potential for growth and our chances of building a future where fishing is an important activity and a pillar of our economy. But it is not just the illegal fishermen who are to blame: Our country knows what is happening, but can do little about it. Lack of resources, lack of technology and lack of effective control have our country tied to a situation that does not seem to be improving in the short term.

The tourism industry

Travelers who have come to Patagonia before were really adventurous. Dirt roads, small and unprepared airports, lack of infrastructure. It was not until the crisis of 2001, when Argentina suffered a huge devaluation, that tourists began to arrive in large numbers, as our country became cheap and competitive compared to other destinations. Thus, little by little, investments in roads began to be paved and new airports were built.

Patagonia's National Parks give this region a number of scenic, natural, and cultural attractions that put it on any traveler's bucket list.

Fortunately, most of the tour guides recognise that the natural and cultural heritage of the region is their way of life and adopt the necessary changes to protect their source of work by raising awareness among visitors. Many of them are also the ones who try to make the local community aware that, if the village in which they live depends to a large extent on tourism, they must do everything possible to preserve the beauty of the place they live in. This is the only way to make an activity sustainable. Not only by delegating responsibility to those who directly impact on the activity, but also to those who indirectly interact with the environment, which is the cornerstone of the industry.

In the case of El Calafate, many colleagues have spoken out against the mega-dams that are still under construction on the historic Santa Cruz river and that may endanger the behavior of the glaciers protected by Los Glaciares National Park.

During the summer in the southern hemisphere, Patagonia receives thousands of tourists from all over the world who want to see live all those stories and photographs that they have consumed for years. It is up to the whole community to care for and protect a very important source of income for the region and for the whole country.

As we have seen, there are various economic activities in Patagonia, but having lived for almost a century dependent on wool monoculture, we cannot speak of a great development of other industries. We can say: Yes, there is oil, but can we say that we manage it well? And so on: coal, energy, fisheries resources, tourism resources, etc.

Let us hope that in the next years we can start thinking in the long term.

The whole of Latin America lives in urgency. It comes out of one and goes into another. This way of life does not allow this region to think about tomorrow, if we are struggling every day with basic issues. And this is how decisions have been taken in the region: on the basis of urgency.

It is necessary to be able to establish state policies that are sustained over time in order to generate economic pillars that do not change according to the trends of the times. Because future generations and the future of our country's economy depend on this. And it is also necessary to invest in research and monitoring.

Investing in Argentina seems like throwing money away. And that also has to change. And control seems to be only a way to have power over others and not to enforce the laws that regulate activities. There is a lack of honesty, a lack of resources, and a lack of investment.

These are the challenges that lie ahead for the Patagonian region, with the dilemma of leaving behind short-term thinking and being able to generate long-term awareness: greater investment, business growth, more jobs, population growth, and much more.

Argentine infantry during the Falklands War (Guerra de Malvinas) in 1982.
Source: *Archivo General de la Nación , AR-AGN-AGAS01-rg-537- Inventario 345487*

CHAPTER 21

Other conflicts in the region

The 20th century was a very complicated one in Latin America. While there were no large-scale wars like those that took place in Europe, the entire region was plunged into political instability. Many countries lived for long years under military dictatorships that disrupted peace and harmony within their borders. These dictatorships generated unnecessary nationalist feelings among the people, accentuating internal pressures and hostility towards neighboring countries.

Six military coups took place during the 20th century in Argentina: in 1930, 1943, 1955, 1962, 1966 and 1976. The latter counted as the darkest and bloodiest in Argentine history, with thousands persecuted, killed, tortured, and disappeared. On the other side of the Andes, Chile has twice been under dictatorship. Under Carlos Ibáñez del Campo, between 1927 and 1931, and under Augusto Pinochet Ugarte, between 1973 and 1990. The latter also had a tone of violence very similar to Argentina's last dictatorial period. But Panama, Nicaragua, Brazil, El Salvador, Uruguay, Paraguay, Peru, Haiti, Honduras, Colombia, Guatemala, the Dominican Republic and Venezuela also had at least one period of military dictatorship.

Returning to Argentina, these military dictatorships' comings and goings increased nationalist sentiments and awakened old rivalries, as, for example, between Argentina and Chile. And although there was supposedly a border agreement signed by both countries, there were always misunderstandings due to misinterpretations. And so a few more conflicts arose during the 20th century.

The *Lago del Desierto* Conflict (1965)

By 1950, aerial surveys of the Andean region had been carried out, which further helped to improve border demarcation. Thanks to these aerial surveys, more accurate maps of the Cordillera region could be made. One of these surveys showed that the area north of the present town of El Chaltén, in the Lago del Desierto area, is part of Argentina. And since there was a Chilean population there, they had been told to regularize the situation, which did not happen immediately.

Years went by and the situation escalated: In October 1965, the Argentine gendarmerie notified the settler Domingo Sepúlveda that he had to regularize his situation. He requested help from the *carabineros* (chilean police) of Lake O'Higgins in Chile, who immediately sent troops to the area.

In those days, the presidents of both countries met, agreeing to the withdrawal of the Chilean carabineros within 48 hours and the resolution of the matter by the Joint Chilean-Argentine Boundary Commission.

In November 1965, there was a confrontation between Argentine and Chilean infantry who were still in the area without knowledge of the order to withdraw, which arrived only the following day. The confrontation resulted in the unfortunate death of Chilean lieutenant Hernán Merino. Weapons, provisions and a Chilean flag that was flying from a makeshift flagpole were seized.

This led to anti-Argentine demonstrations in Santiago de Chile with the burning of flags. In addition, a Chilean plane flew over a ship of the Argentine fleet in Ushuaia at the same time. In the end, an agreement was reached between the parties, which settled the dispute. Chile did not demand Argentina's withdrawal from the area, and the Joint Boundary Commission began its work. In 1967, the Argentine Gendarmerie set up a permanent post to guard Lago del Desierto.

It was not until 1994 that the ruling in favor of Argentina, which retained the area, was made public. But until then it was still an open secret and Argentina decided in 1985 to found the town of El Chaltén very close to the conflict zone, at the foot of the beautiful Torre and Fitz Roy mountains. In 2017, as a gesture of friendship between the two countries, the Argentine government decided to return to Chile the flag seized back in 1965, just for the Day of the Carabinero, in honor of the memory of Lieutenant Hernán Merino, who fell in this confrontation that went down in history as the "Lago del Desierto Conflict".

Argentine soldiers, after lowering the Chilean flag in Laguna del Desierto, proceed to remove it from the flagpole for storage. The flag was returned to Chile in 2017.
Image: Gente Magazine, 1965.

The Beagle Channel Conflict (1978 - 1984)

In December 1978, everything was ready for a war that would have been catastrophic. The timely intervention of John Paul II averted a tragedy that could have marked two brotherly countries forever.

The "Beagle conflict" was a territorial dispute between Argentina and Chile over the demarcation of the eastern mouth of the Beagle Channel, which affected the sovereignty of the Picton, Nueva and Lennox Islands.

This story began in 1971, when the two countries signed an arbitration compromise to settle sovereignty over the islands. An arbitration court ruled in May 1977 that sovereignty was Chilean, which the Argentine dictatorship, headed by dictator Jorge Rafael Videla, was not happy about. In January 1978, Buenos Aires considered the ruling "insanely null and void" and tried, through diplomatic pressure based on its military strength, to force Chile to negotiate. When that plan failed,

"Operation Sovereignty" was launched, the aim of which was to invade Chile and take the islands by force.

Tensions rose, and as both nations prepared for war, by December 1978 pilots from both nations had designated their targets and were about to launch attacks.

War was only averted by a matter of hours. Conflict very nearly broke out and was averted by the mediation of Pope John Paul II.

For both countries and for Latin America as a whole, this potential war would have been catastrophic, for with two military governments, perhaps these islands would be the start of an even larger conflict. A conflict was expected along the entire border, with territory being invaded and then used to swap for territory that might be lost in Patagonia: a madness that could only be orchestrated by two military governments seeking to feed the nationalist sentiment of their people to forget about the other problems at home.

In December 1979 the Pope sent a peace proposal that Argentina rejected. It was not until the democratic government of Raúl Alfonsín that an agreement was reached in Argentina in 1984 ceding to Chile all the territories claimed, namely the Picton, Nueva and Lennox islands and nearby islets, and a zone of economic exclusivity in the Atlantic Ocean.

Map of the area of Beagle Channel and the three island in question.

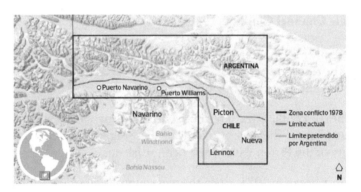

Source: datoposta.com

Dictators Augusto Pinochet for Chile (in white) and Jorge Rafael Videla for Argentina (center) during negotiations that failed in January 1978.
Source: La Nacion newspaper.

The Falklands War or *Guerra de Malvinas* (1982)

The war over the *Malvinas*, fought in the southern autumn of 1982, was a conflict between England and Argentina that lasted just over two months, left some 1,000 dead, and many open wounds. These islands have an important relationship with Patagonia as we saw in the book, being located 650 kilometers from Río Gallegos.

The islands had been occupied by the British since 1833, and Argentina had been insisting on a sovereign claim to the islands, due to their inheritance from the Spanish crown and geographical proximity. There were already talks about shared sovereignty and it seemed that there might be a peaceful solution.

By 1982, the military junta, which had ruled since 1976, was weakened by the growing evidence of human rights violations in a government that left thousands missing people, as well as thousands of dead. It was a dictatorship that tortured, persecuted, censored, and limited citizens' freedoms. On the other hand, the rejection was due to a failed economic policy leading to one of the worst economic crises the country had ever experienced.

A war that would fuel nationalist sentiments could help the military perpetuate itself in power.

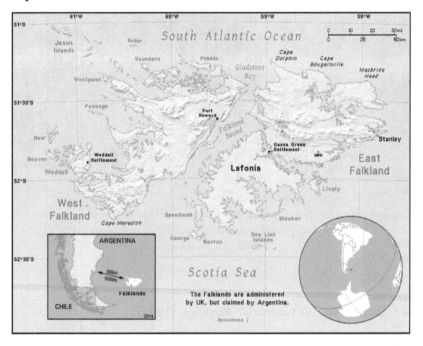

Map of the Falkland/Malvinas islands. *Public domain. Author: Ian Macky*

Initially, the operation received widespread popular support, but the triumphalism was short-lived. And it had little support outside Argentina, beyond that of Latin American countries. The UN condemned the Argentine offensive. The war lasted a total of 72 days, and in June 14th 1982, Argentina signed the unconditional surrender of its troops.

On the Argentine side there were over 700 dead; about 300 on the British side. Many of the Argentine soldiers were ill-trained, ill-equipped, ill-fed, and suffered bullying from their own superiors.

The Argentine defeat resulted to the military government's departure from power, and as the months passed democratic elections were called in December

1983, bringing to an end the bloodiest military dictatorship in Argentina's young history. Although the war ended more about 40 years ago, the territorial conflict remains open and Argentina has not ceased its claim to sovereignty over the islands, whose inhabitants insist that they want to remain British.

Many of these conflicts that we reviewed, claimed the lives of people who died in the line of duty. A duty that is always decided from comfortable desks that will never see what happens on the battlefield. For me, at least these conflicts I have just discussed, were absurdities committed because of the blindness of the leaders in charge.

Hopefully, wars will be a thing of the past and weapons will never again be used as a solution to conflict.

Crucero ARA General Belgrano while sinking after being hit by a British submarine. *Photo: Frigate Lieutenant Martín Sgut.*

Cerro Torre. El Chaltén, Argentina.
Courtesy Juan Pablo Raposo

CHAPTER 22

Mountaineering in the Andes

We are now approaching the end of the book, but before we say goodbye, it is important to know what happened over the mountains with people who have traveled them out of necessity, obligation, or out of their own desire. Today it is many of these mountains and glaciers that attract visitors from all over the world.

The Andes Mountains are some 65 million years old, and were silent witnesses to the changes the region underwent. The rise of these mountains ushered in a new era on Earth, and witnessed the slow fossilization of animal and plant species that disappeared, turning Patagonia into a paleontological paradise for the great variety of fossils that can be found today. Even today we can find marine fossils in the Andes Mountains.

These mountains also witnessed the different ice ages that took place throughout history. Glacier ice is one of the most powerful erosive forces, and it has left its mark on the landscape of the Andes.

These mountains have been at the center of territorial discussions, and also the source of mysteries that have not been solved. The Patagonian Andes were home to animals and peoples who may no longer be with us today. But these same mountains will, for a long time to come, be the natural setting for stories that have yet to be written. The Andes were, are, and will be part of the history of Patagonia.

Mountaineering in Patagonia is an almost inherent activity of the region, whose repetitive steppe landscape is interrupted by the Andes Mountain Range. When talking about mountaineering, we should not only consider professionals who come to the mountainous regions to reach the summits of the area.

In my opinion, we can speak of mountaineering when it comes to physically demanding activities that take place on a mountain.

Based on this last definition, we can say that the native peoples who lived in the Andean environment were mountaineers who acquired the necessary experience to regularly traverse this type of terrain. We could also say that the "conquistadores" who crossed the Andes were mountaineers. We can also include soldiers that for strategic reasons, had to cross the Andes.

But to begin with the "history of mountaineering" I choose to start with the activity of the boundary commissions of both Chile and Argentina. In previous chapters we have mentioned their work in one of the many border conflicts between the two countries.

The Chilean-Argentine Boundary Commission: 1898 - 1909

At the end of the 19th century, Chile and Argentina agreed to peacefully delimit their borders. To this end, both nations were faced with the need to duly map thousands of kilometers of Andean border. For this purpose these new commissions were created: the Chilean Boundary Commission, and its equivalent, the Argentinean. It was agreed, after the work of Argentine explorer Francisco Pascasio Moreno, that the border line would run along the high peaks that divide the waters.

Both commissions worked on both sides of their respective territories, usually independently of each other, but often together. These commissions were made up of engineers, geographers, and experts from different disciplines, while some "explorers" served as guides to help the groups survive.

The Commission's task was to mark with milestones all the passes of the Cordillera at the intersection of each of them with the dividing line. To locate them, it was first necessary to map the entire mountain range, which he was able to do in several years and on maps at a scale of 1:250,000.

At the border crossings, four-meter-high iron milestones, built on a skeleton of iron bars and plates, were set in concrete bases. All-important topographical stations were also photographed.

Field work took place between 1896 and the end of 1909, and between the two nations they were able to erect more than 500 milestones.

This task of study and demarcation carried out by these commissions took a long time and inspired the wave of mountaineers who would gradually begin to arrive in Patagonia. The boom would come after the Second World War.

The boundary commissions of both countries were to measure and erect the boundary markers between Argentina and Chile. They were made in agreement between both parties.
Source: cancillería.gob.ar

An Italian priest on the Andes:

Alberto Maria de Agostini was born in Piemonte at the end of the 19th century. Growing up in a mountainous environment during his young years gave him a great passion for the peaks that surrounded him. He developed an intrepid adventurous spirit that took him to places where only very few had been able to go. In 1909 he was ordained as a priest in the Salesian Order and this opened the door for him to reach one of the most inhospitable places on the planet: Tierra del Fuego, in Patagonia.

The Salesians had been in Tierra del Fuego since 1893 and had founded a settlement with the aim of gathering and "civilizing" the Selk'nam and protecting them from the threat posed by the gold prospectors, and mainly the ranchers, who promoted a policy of extermination against the Selk'nams who resisted colonization, stealing sheep and destroying wire fences that reduced the free passage of the original inhabitants of these lands.

In 1910, Agostini arrived in Patagonia and in his free time he dedicated himself to doing what he had been passionate about since he was a child: climbing mountains. Thus began the legacy of this Italian in the region, climbing Mount Olivia, which is located in the surroundings of Ushuaia. This first summit was the start of a successful climbing life in the region: mixing his religious life and his passionate hobby, Agostini will be remembered more than anything else for his legacy as a mountaineer and explorer.

In Chile he took part in more than twenty expeditions, while in Argentina he also undertook many others: many of the names adopted by the regions he explored have some reference to Italy or religion. His legacy is so great that his best photographs of mountains and native populations are still used today as a reference for the study of this incredible landscape: the book *Andes Patagonicos* is a masterpiece in the study of Patagonian history, as well as in geography, botany and anthropology.

In Chile he traveled to the Torres del Paine area, while in Argentina he was contracted for an exploration for the future opening of Los Glaciares National Park, reaching the summit of Cerro Mayo and the northern arm of Lago Argentino where he would walk on the Upsala Glacier. There he discovered the peaks of Cerro Roma and Cerro Don Bosco, names that come from his italian roots.

Father Agostini is known in Chile as *Padre Patagonia*, although in Argentina he has not had such widespread recognition. Agostini's legacy can be seen, as we said, in his publications through which he made the Patagonian mountains known in Europe, which motivated other climbers to turn their eyes to this region of the planet. Of his photographic and filmic records of the region, those of native peoples stand out, forming a valuable testimony of ethnic groups that have disappeared today. At the same time, he was a pioneer in taking aerial photographs of the Southern Patagonian Ice Field, which have been of great importance for the mapping of the area. He was a pioneer in the use of color photography, in accordance with the most modern technologies of the time. His films, on the other hand, constitute a legacy of immense value, since they are the first and only cinematographic records of the Magellanic peoples and of the region in general. The most important of these are *Tierra del Fuego* and *Tierras Magallánicas* which can be found on YouTube.

Local institutions

Both Chile and Argentina began to take the sport with the seriousness it deserved, and on both sides of the Andes Mountain Range the first "Andean clubs" were born with the great European influence that had discovered this wonderful region.

San Carlos de Bariloche is the name of the city where the first Argentine Andean Club was born. This place is located in Northern Patagonia, in the province of Rio Negro, and a small store called "*La Alemana*" (the German) used to operate there, in honor of the German colony that had settled in the area. The owner of the store was called Carlos Wiederholtd and he had a great talent for business and for facilitating the development of the community where he lived, turning his store into an indispensable business and meeting center for the region.

One day, Carlos received a letter from abroad: in the old days it was common to find the prefix "don" as "Don Juan" or "Don José" to speak of an owner or "señor" who owned some land or establishment. This letter appeared to be addressed to "Don Carlos", the owner of the warehouse, but a mistake in the spelling meant that it read "San Carlos" (like *saint*). This was much to the amusement of the recipient of the message who proudly displayed it to visitors to the store; in time he renamed his store "San Carlos". Eventually with the growth of the settlement around this store, the town itself was named San Carlos de Bariloche: adding the place where this "saint" can be found - the Vuriloche pass, the original name of the pass between the mountains connecting Chile and Argentina.

Because of this close relationship with the Andes Mountains, the first Andean club in Argentina was founded in 1931: the Club Andino de Bariloche. It was founded by Otto Meiling, Emilio Frey, Reinaldo Knapp, and Juan Neumeyer, who brought the necessary experience from Switzerland and Germany for the proper development of this entity. In the course of time, branches were established in the rest of the Andean region, both in Chile and Argentina, motivating locals and welcoming visitors to develop guided activities in the region.

Members of the Club Andino Bariloche in the Cerro Lopez hut, ca. 1947.
Courtesy: Federico Silín. Colección Hartung en Archivo Visual Patagónico.

In 1951, the Instituto Nacional del Hielo Continental Patagónico (something like "glacial ice institute") was born in Argentina, also formed by members of these Andean clubs, whose mission was to establish shelters in the vicinity of the glaciers in order to carry out a closer study of them. This institution has also stood out for crossing the Southern Patagonian Ice Field and supporting the Argentine Air Force in its landing practices on the Upsala glacier.

Unfortunately, the "Instituto del Hielo" lost prominence when these glacier studies and measurements started to be made by means of photogrammetric flights: i.e.

they are measured by means of aerial photographs, comparing them with old photos (e.g. with Father Agostini's photos).

Today the shelters built by this institute are still standing, but they lack the necessary care and maintenance. In 2019, together with a group of friends, we restored the identification plate to the "Refugio Pascale" near the Upsala Glacier and Estancia Cristina. This badge was in the Estancia Cristina Museum for more than 30 years for unknown reasons, and in my initiative as Curator of this Museum we contacted the Argentine Chancellery (which is in charge of the Ice Institute) to ask for their authorization to return it to where it belongs.

Members of the Institute of Ice on the Ice Field (1953)
Source: Archivo del Instituto Nacional del Hielo Continental Patagónico.

Cesare Maestri and the Cerro Torre:

Cesare Maestri was born in 1929 in the Italian city of Trento. He was born surrounded by his beloved Alps, which will mark his destiny forever.

In 1943, after the German occupation of northern Italy, his father was condemned to death and they fled to Ferrara, only to return to Trento when the war ended. Looking for a way to overcome his wartime experiences, he took up climbing, and from then on and for the rest of his life, he devoted himself almost exclusively to mountaineering.

Cesare Maestri
Source: Campioni dello Sport
1969/70-n. 9

Thanks to his climbing ability he became a great local icon. His climbing techniques were unique and carried over into the traditional climbing teachings of the region. He was baptized "the spider of the Dolomites".

In 1958 he arrived in Patagonia to climb Cerro Torre with an Italian-Argentine commission. In that expedition it was decided that the ascent of Cerro Torre "is impossible".

First ascent of Cerro Torre (1959)

A year later, Maestri and the Austrian Toni Egger (who was one of the best ice climbers of the time) plus a support team including his friend Cesarino Fava, arrived to make the first ascent of Cerro Torre in 1959.

Egger and Maestri were lost without trace for some six days, presumably on the east face of Cerro Torre. When the support team led by their friend Fava went out to meet the pair, they found only a dying Maestri. Descending from the summit, an avalanche took Egger by surprise during the victorious descent. Maestri had survived after a lonely march that left him on the verge of collapse. But, according to Maestri, they had reached the summit. The evidence, sadly, was lost forever in the camera Egger was carrying.

The east face of Cerro Torre is a granite wall topped by an ice mushroom. Maestri always pointed out that a layer of ice covered the east face that year and that his was an ascent on ice, hence there was no trace of his passage.

In Italy he received recognition for his bravery and signed valuable contracts for the publication of his books. He received the approval of his fellow mountaineers: they hailed Maestri and Egger as having accomplished *"the greatest climbing feat of all time"*. It is important to remember that after the Second World War, Italy needed to lift the spirits of a population mired in the tragic consequences of the war. This kind of news vindicated Italian sentiment.

In 1968, an English expedition to Cerro Torre attempted an ascent by a theoretically simpler route. Given the impossibility, Maestri's account began to be questioned. The opinion of this expedition was picked up by the English magazine *Mountain*, which ended up publishing a report of Maestri's ascent, in which the "weak" parts of his account were highlighted, suggesting the falsity of the story. In Patagonia, subsequent attempts to repeat the route to climb the Torre triggered suspicions and discredit began to be associated with the Maestri surname.

Second ascent of Cerro Torre (1970)

Cesare Maestri always maintained that he and Egger had reached the summit in 1959. Egger had been swept away by an avalanche while descending and lost his camera photos with him. The inconsistencies in Maestri's account, and the lack of spikes, pitons or fixed ropes on the route, have led most of the mountaineering community to doubt Maestri's account.

To put an end to these accusations, the proud Maestri decided to return to Cerro Torre in 1970, now as a devotee of artificial climbing, and achieved the impossible: to generate a second, tremendously controversial, ascent of Cerro Torre. To overcome the challenge offered by the rock, Maestri's Italian team brought a compressor to drill into the rock and place nails for belaying and climbing.

With the help of this fuel-powered compressor, Maestri equipped 350 meters of rock with expansion spikes and reached the end of the rocky part of the mountain, just below an ice mushroom that covers the summit. Maestri claimed that the ice mushroom is not part of the mountain and therefore he did not continue the ascent. The group led by Maestri left the compressor there, tied to the last nails, a hundred meters below the summit. The route that Maestri followed is today known as the *compressor route* and was subsequently climbed in 1979 by Jim Bridwell, confirming the feat. Today it is not considered a complete ascent unless you reach the summit mushroom to its highest point.

And so, a second controversy was written on Cerro Torre.

Maestri continued climbing and, to his regret, these doubts always haunted him. Once settled in Italy, he spent the rest of his years running a gastronomic establishment and working as a mountain guide. He wrote books and always offered to give talks and interviews, although everything always seemed to take him back to his experiences in Patagonia.

In the absence of irrefutable evidence, no one can say categorically that Maestri lied, even if his story is full of shadows. It is unimaginable that the life of a gifted climber would be tarnished for decades. For him, his truth he defended with courage and struggle, but his reputation was drilled by tiny spikes with a single question: *"Did you really climb Cerro Torre?"*

About Cerro Torre and Patagonia's most emblematic mountains

It is located between Argentina in the province of Santa Cruz and Chile in the Magallanes region. It is 3,102 meters high, and lies on the eastern border of the Southern Patagonian Ice Field. It is a granite spire crowned by an impressive ice mushroom, a product of the freezing of moisture brought by the violent winds from the Pacific. The quickest access is through El Chaltén, an Argentinean town founded in 1985 for geopolitical reasons near *Lago del Desierto*. This town today has become a place of great tourist importance visited by mountaineers, hikers and travelers from all over the world.

It is not the only great Patagonian mountain, but is neighboring Mount Fitz Roy, another great Patagonian postcard of the Argentinean sector.

As mentioned, behind these mountains lies the Southern Patagonian Ice Field: the third largest icefield in the world. After Antarctica and Greenland, the Southern Patagonian Ice Field is the third largest ice mass on our planet.

On the Pacific Ocean side, the Torres del Paine is another beautiful place that invites tourists to discover these beautiful corners of Patagonia.

These imposing, majestic, and above all peaceful and silent places sometimes lack a voice to tell us these particular stories that took place in Patagonia. There are countless stories related to mountaineering that I had to omit due to the nature of the book, but I have chosen some of the most representative ones to try to convey how the activity has grown in recent times and the importance it has in the region.

Cerro Torre from the air. You can appreciate the ice mushroom on the top. Torre glacier and Torre lagoon can also be seen. From that lagoon El Chalten is only 9 km. away.
Photography kindly shared by Alejandro Jaimes

Estancia Cristina Lodges.
Courtesy Juan Pablo Raposo.

CHAPTER 23

The Masters family in Patagonia

Patagonia, still desolate and wild today, shows us that the immigrants who came to this region back when it was needed the most deserve special consideration. Like the Welsh colony, each of these newcomers had to struggle with desert soil, a total lack of communications and the deprivations of such latitudes. This required the highest doses of willpower to overcome any obstacle.

For me, these immigrants, also called pioneers, are the ones who gave Patagonia its new character after facing the extraordinary task of reaching the farthest corners of the world to put down roots in a land that resisted them.

We will review the history of the Masters family, which inspired me to write this book.

In the process I realized that if I was to tell their story, I also had to explain different historical processes in the Patagonian region to better understand the magnitude of this family history. Therefore, I decided to compile this book with the different historical processes that took place in Patagonia in chronological order in order to have a better grasp of how the different events unfolded.

In these chapters, the development of the life of the Masters family is also chronological and I hope you can see how all the different historical processes we discussed in our book will cross the life of this single family in the middle of the endless Patagonia.

Percival and Jessie Masters in Patagonia (1900)

Percival Joseph Masters was born in 1876, in Lymington, Hampshire, England.

In his youth he had been a sailor for four years on a ship called Rhouma. After several visits to Punta Arenas, on the Strait of Magellan, he returned to England with the intention of moving to these distant lands. Having visited the Patagonian region in 1900, he had seen the possibilities that both Argentina and Chile presented to those who wished to settle in these latitudes.

This sailor convinced his fiancée Elizabeth "Jessie" Wildig, whom he married, to leave for the south of the planet.

Percival and Jessie arrive in Rio Gallegos in the province of Santa Cruz in Argentina. Neither of them had any experience in farming or ranching, so they first get a job at a post on the Estancia El Condor: "The Gap" is an important section of the Estancia, close to Cabo Virgenes, which forms a huge ditch that drops down to a cliff coastline.

By 1900 the owners of the ranch were the Waldron brothers and the Wood brothers, cousins to each other. There, Percival Masters became a sheep herder and there his two children were born, Herbert, on May 14th , 1902 and Cristina, on August 4th , 1904.

From left to right: Percival, Jessie, Herbert and Cristina Masters.
Courtesy: Estancia Cristina Sociedad Anónima.

After several seasons of work, the family wanted to be able to start their own Estancia and left the security of working at *El Condor* to seek their own destiny.

We remember that in Patagonia, it was very common for land to be given to immigrants who wished to work. The big problem was that by 1904 almost all the land near the Atlantic coast was occupied. The chances of obtaining land lay to the west, some 300 to 400 kilometers from the sea, and almost at the foot of the Andes Mountains. This meant weeks of distance between the sea and the mountains. But it also meant the possibility of realizing a dream, and this was even stronger: with their newborn baby Cristina, they set off on a long and tortuous wagon journey to the Lago Argentino area, carrying a handful of sheep.

El Calafate and Lago Argentino area (1904 - 1914)

They arrived at Cerro Frias, near the present-day city of El Calafate, in the last months of 1904, and went as far as Lake Roca, where they stayed for a short time.

After spending several years in the Cerro Frias area, in 1907, Percival Masters wrote a letter to the Governor of the territory, requesting formal permission to occupy the area, as he and his family had been living there for three years, giving details of its location with a sketch. Unfortunately, this request was not taken granted. We have to point out that corruption and "friendships" between politicians and companies often denied opportunities to small farmers. Because of this, they had to move.

The family has a brief stay in the town of El Calafate, but without success. In May 1908 they arrived at a new site: the Río Bote on the outskirts of El Calafate.

Once settled here, they started working again, this time with a good number of sheep and more men. They raised chickens, built a shed to work with the sheep, bathed them, sold some animals, carried on the shearing, chased pumas, and they had relations with numerous ranchers.

But once again, circumstances were adverse and they had to leave.

With several years of experience behind them, the Masters family did not want to give up. They move to a place called Punta Bandera: a natural harbor on Lake Argentino. Here, in 1877, Perito Moreno raised the Argentine flag after the expedition that followed in the footsteps of Darwin and Fitz Roy, up the Santa Cruz River to a huge lake that Perito Moreno named "Lago Argentino".

They arrived there in 1910, and stayed there for three years, using a rowing boat and a flatbed to transport sheep and horses to different places on the lake: the Avellaneda peninsula and the Herminita peninsula. This last place is near the Upsala Glacier and there is a natural bay that seems to be very fertile. This bay was visited by an Englishman called Hesketh Prichard who was looking for an almost "mythological" animal: the Mylodon. Could this bay be their new home?

Foundation of Estancia Masters (1914)

After numerous attempts, the Masters family settled on the far shore of the northern arm of Lago Argentino in 1914.

Once settled in this bay, they had no choice but to live in tents. Eventually they built a precarious house of stone and mud. This house would later be made of sheet metal and wood. They prepared a small plot of land and planted an *alameda*, a line of poplars to protect themselves from the winds.

Despite the harsh climate, it did not take long for new "settlers" to emerge who also coveted these fields and submitted applications for occupation which, behind the scenes, were oiled with fluid public relations.

The small settlers, always vulnerable, had to protect themselves from the economic interests of the large corporations that accumulated land exponentially. For this reason, in the northern area of Lake Argentino, a partnership was formed between Percival Masters and other lake settlers to organize the livestock farming activities in this area, which Masters would carry out from his Estancia.

They would work together for a few years, and then eventually the Masters would take over the management of the current Estancia.

Once the permits to stock and graze the flocks were granted, the fundamental problem for the new occupants of the Estancia Masters was to obtain the sheep to increase production.

Although the first sheep arrived in Santa Cruz transported by sailing ships from the Falkland Islands, from then on, cattle, horses and sheep arrived in successive drives, organized by private initiatives as we have read in the chapter on The Great Sheep Drive. To bring the sheep to the Estancia Masters the family had to cross the sheep by boat to the other side of Lake Argentino and then herd them over mountain terrain for several days against the wind, the cold, and the hungry pumas of the area.

Early years of Estancia Masters.
Courtesy: Estancia Cristina Sociedad Anónima.

The most important steamer on Lake Argentino: César (1916)

It should be noted that there were some boats and rowing boats on the lake. But a lake of more than fifteen hundred square kilometers needed something more appropriate.

In the Pampa it is impossible to imagine a gaucho without a horse. And a family living in isolation at the northern end of Argentina's largest lake could not do without a boat.

At that time, wool production only relied on shipping as a means of transport in the lake area. Once these had been overcome, the means of transport from the estancias to the ocean was the ox-drawn cart or *chata*. To move the wool to the Atlantic coast, caravans of *chatas* were formed.

From the estancias, they had to go around the big lake to continue with their bundles to Río Gallegos, and on their return, they brought with provisions for the long winter seasons.

The time taken for this ground travel from Lago Argentino to Rio Gallegos was at best one month.

Percival Masters then had a boat brought from Buenos Aires. The steamer named *Cesar* was transported overland from the Atlantic coast with twenty oxen pulling a structure mounted on solid wooden wheels. The expedition took several weeks, and at the estancia they finished assembling some of the pieces.

Once on the lake, it was not only the Masters and their wool that were transported; animals, hides, everything passed through the César. Travelers who wanted to reach the estancia could only rely on this vessel. Soon after its arrival, the steamer had become a reference point on Lake Argentino. This steamer also supported a sawmill project that took place on Lake Argentino and many travelers and explorers such as Father De Agostini traveled on it during their exploratory periods.

César sailed tirelessly on Lake Argentino until the 1960s.

César saling Lago Argentino.
Courtesy Estancia Cristina Sociedad Anónima.

About the sons:

Although little is known about them, it is very useful to understand the tortuous journey from their birth to finding the place where they settled with their family. There they went, where no one had dared.

In 1914, and when already in the new Estancia, Herbert was eleven years old and Cristina was only nine years old. The tasks were many and they both showed a willingness to work.

Three years after arriving in the area, in 1916, Herbert was sent to study at Saint George's College in the south of Buenos Aires. This was a boarding school, where the children spent several years receiving the necessary education: not only basic education, but also workshops in various trades. After several years he returned to Estancia. He never left again. The villagers called him "*Don Alberto*" as Herbert is not really catchy in the Spanish language.

Cristina always wanted to work alongside her father, and soon she was involved in every task on the farm. She went out into the fields, stumbled around and also took part in the shearing season. Once they had settled on the northern arm of Lago Argentino, when the family seemed to have built a safe place for the children, Cristina died in 1924.

The cause was pneumonia in her early 20s, and there was no doctor in the vicinity. Cristina Masters, who had managed to create an unparalleled bond with the Estancia and especially with her father Percival, fell victim to the isolation. This isolation translates into loneliness and is made worse by the cold and the wind. These factors make Patagonia a land that refuses to be tamed. That is why this battle must be fought day after day, and one must never let one's guard down.

Cristina Masters passed away in 1924 and the estancia will remember this by renaming itself *Estancia Cristina*.

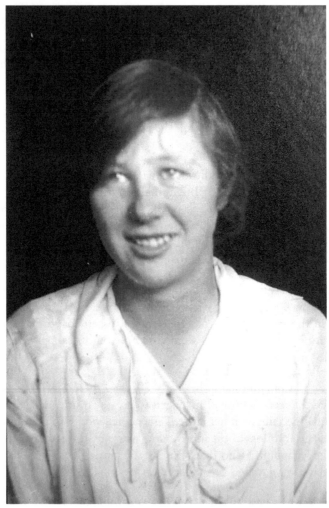

Cristina Masters.
Courtesy: Estancia Cristina Sociedad Anónima.

The year was 1924, the family was then one member short, but they still had 12,000 sheep, 20,000 hectares and a boat to take care of. The lease they had in force was due to expire in 1944, when they could obtain ownership of this land forever and finally fulfill their dream. The wool was still profitable and the future promising.

Herbert Masters ca. 1930.
Courtesy: Estancia Cristina
Sociedad Anónima.

CHAPTER 24

Estancia Cristina

In the middle of nowhere, the Masters family was able to choose their destiny. Some things they could not foresee, such as the death of their daughter from pneumonia. The first doctor of Lago Argentino arrived only in 1935: Dr. José Formenti. He decided to seek new horizons knowing that quality medical care was not abundant in Patagonia. There were no supplies or instruments, almost everything was his own equipment to attend to the people of the town that grew and grew.

This hard loss in 1924 led to a change in the name of their estancia. But what they could not change was their spirit, which has allowed them to overcome all kinds of obstacles.

Estancia Cristina radio amateurs

In the 1920s Herbert Masters had returned from studying in Buenos Aires and brought with him the idea of setting up an amateur radio station on the Estancia. This idea of being radio amateurs would later become a family tradition.

The radio played a fundamental role for intercommunication on the ranches, given their isolation throughout the southern Patagonian region.

Not only were there radio amateurs as in the Masters family, but there were radio stations that would broadcast messages at fixed times so that workers and inhabitants of remote rural areas would only listen to the radio at those times. The messages were of vital importance in times of rain or snowfall.

In order to generate electricity in rural areas, a 6-volt generator called *Wincharger* was imported from the USA: this invention would provide enough power for a 6-volt radio transmitter and for house lights thanks to a removable battery. The patagonian wind became their ally on this occasion.

Correspondence

The mailboxes were usually located on the side of the road, miles away from the main house, so it was the job of an employee to stop by to see if the postman had left anything for the mailboxes to receive.

In the case of the Masters family letterbox, it was located at Punta Bandera on the shore of Lago Argentino. This mailbox was very large and made of an oil barrel. It was normal for them not to go very often to pick up their mail given the distance, so the accumulation of packages and magazines to which they had subscriptions, such as National Geographic and Popular Mechanics, made it necessary to think of a large mailbox.

Other practices that existed were the overflights to drop mail, and for this reason many estancias painted their names large on their roofs so that the pilot could easily locate them.

Example of a mailbox from an Estancia called La Maria. Located in Puerto San Julian.
Photo from Mabel Medina.

Left: Antenna of the Estancia Cristina radio station around 1980.
Right: Model of "Wincharger" that Estancia Cristina had.
Courtesy: Estancia Cristina Sociedad Anónima.

The creation of the National Park Los Glaciares (1937)

In the 1930s, the National Parks Administration led a series of exploratory trips in the Patagonian mountain range area for the creation of new parks: a commission was entrusted with the area between Lago Argentino and Lago San Martín and was entrusted to the Salesian priest and explorer De Agostini, whom we know from the previous chapters.

After these explorations, four national parks were created in Argentina, one of which is Los Glaciares National Park.

According to the law, all land declared as a National Park belongs to the National State and no private properties are allowed. With this in mind, the Estancia Cristina was inside the perimeter of the new National Park.

The Masters family were still in the middle of their lease. This means that they were still tenants and not owners. The Masters would have needed only 7 more years of work to conclude that lease and own the land. Land that, in 1937, was within the territory delimited by the National Park. In short: the creation of Los Glaciares National Park interrupted this lease. The Masters Family will not be able to become the owners of the Estancia Cristina. And their dream seems to be crumbling. Worse still... they may have to be evicted.

But the situation of the Masters was not unique. Many other Estancias that existed prior to the creation of the National Parks in Patagonia were in a similar dilemma. For this reason, the National Parks decided to present a "solution" to all these occupants. The environmental impact of livestock grazing in these areas was the main debate.

With the creation of the National Park, regulations were created to conserve the protected areas. The number of animals had to be declared by each Estancia year after year with the promise of gradually reducing their presence within the Park. Life itself needed to be regulated. The Park Service enforced permits for boating and sailing on the lakes and rivers. Logging was banned as an economic activity, leaving only the use of trees for heating.

Hunting of pumas and foxes was strictly forbidden. It should be remembered that they were normally hunted to protect the animals on the ranches, such as sheep. The number of dogs on the ranches was also controlled, as dogs are the main harassers of the native fauna.

Permission to occupy

In order to find a legal solution, it was then proposed to recognize these settlers by means of "occupation and grazing permits", with the idea of encouraging them to replace their traditional activities with the provision of tourism services or other activities aligned with the objectives in the protected areas. In this type of permit, it was established that these rights would be non-transferable and would only serve until the end of the descendance of each family.

With this permission, the fate of the Masters family was sealed, which by this time consisted of Percival, Jessie and Herbert, who by 1937 was still single.

Life at Estancia Cristina

Sheep farming was the main source of income, but with the pressure from the Park Service it was no longer possible to keep so many animals. The fewer animals there were, the less wool was produced on the ranch. Also, the price of wool was gradually dropping for several reasons: the Panama Canal, which replaced the Strait of Magellan, and the appearance of synthetic fabrics. These events caused the price of wool to fall worldwide and also for Patagonia to stop being relevant for the trade.

On the other hand, Percival was already retiring from the leading role due to his advanced age, leaving Herbert in charge of the operation at Estancia Cristina.

Given the dryness of the land, it was imperative to have a constant irrigation system to keep an orchard with the fruits and vegetables for the family's consumption. They needed to grow and water the poplars and pines used to protect the garden of the main house from the strong winds. In 1945 a water wheel (*noria*) was built to raise water from the Caterina River and channel it to the orchard, garden, houses and facilities. This waterwheel, although it had to be rebuilt, can still be seen today at Estancia Cristina.

Waterwheel of Estancia Cristina towards 1980.
Courtesy: Estancia Cristina Sociedad Anónima.

The Caterina River runs through the whole valley of Estancia Cristina and its water gave the Masters the vitality to face each day in this small corner of Patagonia. Its water comes from the glaciers of the Andes and close to Estancia Cristina lies the Upsala Glacier, one of the largest in the Southern Patagonian Ice Field. This glacier will be of vital importance in the coming years, as many expeditions will start or finish at Estancia Cristina.

The Mountains and Glaciers of Estancia Cristina (1953-1962)

In 1952, Mario Bertone had concluded his expedition to the Patagonian Ice Field representing Argentina and after this event the creation of the National Institute of Patagonian Continental Ice was decreed (mentioned in chapter 23).

The Institute was created to closely study the region's glaciers and Bertone became its coordinator. Later, he was a member of the study commissions that carried out glaciological research, and stimulated aerial photogrammetric survey work, technically and scientifically studying the Patagonian glaciers.

In 1953, a dozen shelters were built to get as close as possible to the glaciers. The first shelter they installed was called Upsala, on the west side of the glacier of the same name, which is accessed by the Cristina arm of Lake Argentino. This metal shelter, covered with zinc sheets and with a wooden interior to better insulate against the cold, was installed without the use of helicopters, since the army sent a battalion of four hundred men who made their way from Estancia Cristina to the shelter. These constructions are inside the Estancia Cristina and can still be seen.

Upsala shelter towards 1960.
Source: Archivo del Instituto Nacional del Hielo Continental Patagónico.

In another chapter we have talked about Antarctica, and Estancia Cristina has a close relationship with this continent. The conditions and characteristics of the Patagonian Ice Field are as harsh and extreme as those prevailing in Antarctica, but with the undeniable advantage of almost permanent communication with the rest of the country at all times of the year.

The access to the Patagonian Ice Field is through the Upsala Glacier, which is only a few kilometers away from the buildings of Estancia Cristina.

This glacier is almost sixty kilometers long, and its surface was lashed by meteorological phenomena, which at these heights and latitudes have a violence and magnitude similar to the most rigorous polar weather. This confirmed that it is the most suitable environment for replicating the Antarctic environment, particularly in terms of climate, geology and topography.

For these reasons, Argentina then considered, through the Air Force, that the Upsala Glacier area was the best place to perform trainings. The goal was to make its presence effective in such a difficult-to-access environment.

All this background, favorable for good pre-Antarctic training, led to the start of "Operation Upsala", which took place in May 1962 at the Estancia Cristina.

"Operation Upsala" (1962)

The Argentine Air Force had orders to improve its presence in Antarctica, changing the way Argentina was connected to the "white continent". Their idea was to be able to land planes in Antarctica over a terrain with extreme weather conditions in order to improve communication and to guarantee the relief of personnel, even in the event of emergencies. For this reason, it was necessary to practice how to achieve this type of landings and to practice in a place with similar conditions, and so the Upsala Glacier was chosen.

Herbert Masters was the guide for an Air Force ground party that had to walk over the glacier until a suitable landing site could be found and marked. At almost sixty years of age, Herbert was able to accomplish this task without any inconvenience.

The operation was completed and everything was ready for the Douglas model C-47 TC-33 aircraft to land successfully on the Upsala Glacier on June 7th, 1962.

TC-33 aircraft landed on the Upsala glacier.
Source: Archivo del Instituto Nacional del Hielo Continental Patagónico.

Another great story that took place at the incredible Estancia Cristina: At Estancia Cristina, this ground party also built a 600 meter-long runway where Cessna aircrafts performed relieving duties.

A Cessna 180 aircraft, registration number LQ-ZKF, descended from the Lago Argentino aerodrome, breaking the isolation of the area. According to witnesses, the Masters could not hold back their tears when they saw the arrival of an aircraft at the Estancia.

Operations continued for a few years and then they left the site to start activities in Antarctica. With the departure of the Air Force who were present for several summers accompanying the Masters, there is a gap that will gradually be filled by other visitors. Mountain lovers who started arriving to this "paradise" to explore the beautiful geography of the Andes.

We remember that Estancia Cristina had fewer and fewer animals, Percival and Jessie were already very old and with Herbert taking over the economic activities of the place, the hourglass was about to decree the end of a story that was written in that occupancy permit granted by the National Parks Administration.

Boat "Cristina" built at the Estancia thanks to the blueprints of the magazine "Popular Mechanics".
Courtesy Juan Pablo Raposo.

CHAPTER 25

The end and a new beginning

Overcoming distance and loneliness was one of the most constant challenges for the men and women who struggled to adapt to an environment as hostile and remote as Patagonia.

The Masters, living so far away from the world in an area surrounded by water, mountains and glaciers, had to find a way to reconnect with the society around them. That is why they had brought César: the steamer that tirelessly sailed the Lago Argentino.

A trip from Estancia Cristina to the major port on Lago Argentino (Punta Bandera) took twelve to fourteen hours each way. The steamer was already quite worn out by the years and Herbert decided it was time for a change.

In the context that wool was no longer so profitable, the economic situation was no longer good enough to simply order a new boat, they had to adjust to the new reality. The Masters received monthly *Popular Mechanics* magazines, and in some issues, they were able to find a step-by-step guide to building a boat.

Herbert and a very skilled employee by the name of Mansilla then set about the task of replacing the steamer, which had been in service for more than 40 years.

It took several years, but finally the new boat was finished in the makeshift carpentry shop that occupied one wing of the shearing shed. The new boat needed an engine, and this was ordered from the United States. With this new boat they were able to shorten the journey times to a mere four hours per leg. The new boat was named "*Cristinita*" in honor of the never forgotten daughter of the family.

The ship sailed until the 1990s, and today rests on the shores of Lago Argentino near the main house of Estancia Cristina.

Janet Hermingston: a new inhabitant of the Estancia

In March 1966, the Scotswoman Janet Hermingston arrived on the Cristina. Born south of Edinburgh, she had gone to Tierra del Fuego as a child with her father and family. During their stay in Patagonia, the First World War broke out and they decided to stay for good.

Janet grew up, married, and was widowed by Mr. Mac Donald at a very young age.

Janet arrived at Estancia Cristina looking for new horizons and with the idea of fulfilling the task of caretaker for Percival and Jessie, who were at a very advanced age. On arrival, she was immediately captivated by the place and got on well with the family members, being a great help to Herbert in the house.

At Estancia Cristina, she was to be Jessie Masters' helper on the doctor's orders. Gradually, she became an active part of the administration of Estancia Cristina, helping Herbert in numerous tasks related to the sheep-farming activity of the place. Finally, Jessie died aged 95 in 1971, and Percival Masters, the Estancia's founder, died in 1977 aged 101.

Janet Hermingston in Estancia Cristina.
Source: Estancia Cristina Sociedad Anónima.

Mountaineers and Estancia Cristina

After the Air Force surveys and the construction of shelters in the Andes Mountains between the 50's and 60's, the first climbers started to arrive at Estancia Cristina. They were welcomed by the family who were eager to meet people from other countries with a sense of adventure.

In the 1960s, the legendary English climber Eric Shipton was already carrying the world's most important climbs in his backpack.

He met the Masters and set off to explore the glaciers in the area. All these expeditions provided Shipton with the experience he wanted to gather to attempt a more ambitious crossing of the southern geography: crossing the Southern Patagonian Ice Field, which he accomplished in almost two months.

Special mention should be made of the explorations and first ascents made in the Southern Andes by the brothers Jorge and Pedro Skvarca. Born in what is now the Republic of Slovenia, they emigrated to Argentina in 1956. After gaining experience in the mountains of Bariloche, they started an intense sporting and scientific career in the Southern Patagonian Ice Field. Although at that time the attention of the most renowned climbers in the world was focused on the Fitz Roy and Torre mountains, as we saw in another chapter of the book, the Skvarca brothers went to very little explored areas, located to the west of San Martín-O'Higgins, Viedma and Argentino lakes. There they climb numerous virgin peaks, particularly in the vicinity of the Upsala Glacier.

Pedro Skvarca on a crossing of the Ice Field in 1976.
Image: Tecnoduque – own work, CC BY-SA 4.0 via Wikimedia Commons

They climbed several peaks together, such as Cerro Norte at Estancia Cristina. Here they spent several summers living with the Masters family.

Besides being an excellent climber, Pedro is considered one of the most renowned glaciologists in Argentina. He is a privileged witness of the dramatic changes that the Upsala Glacier underwent after 1966.

For two decades he has been studying the impact of climate change on the ice masses of Antarctica and Patagonia. He is a member of the International Glaciological Society, Academician of the National Academy of Geography, and Director of the Glaciarium, Museum of patagonian Ice.

Casimiro Ferrari, for his part, began his attempts to climb Cerro Murallón here in 1979. He spent several years in the Caterina valley until 1984, when he finally reached the summit with his companions Paolo Vitali and Carlo Aldé.

During the 1960s and 1970s, several Argentinean expeditions to the great snow-capped peaks passed through the area.

It was Casimiro Ferrari who also climbed Cerro Torre for the first time, if one does not take into account Cesare Maestri's ascent.

The last years (1982-1997)

The Panama Canal was the beginning of the end, and Patagonia knew it all along, but did nothing to make its product competitive. The wool did not require a special preservation process and was in high demand on the world market. This led to an interesting profitability of sheep farming which justified wool monoculture.

Then, the substitution of wool by synthetic fibers reduced world demand for this commodity, which led to a continuous fall in the international price. In addition, fixed costs increased, leading to a progressive fall in producers' net income.

In 1982 Herbert and Janet got married because of their mutual companionship of so many years and also to prevent Janet from being evicted in case of any eventuality happening to Herbert. We recall that the occupancy permit authorized only the founding family to live in the house without the possibility of sale or transfer of rights.

Herbert and Janet Masters.
Courtesy: Estancia Cristina Sociedad Anónima.

Only two years later, Herbert Masters died at the Estancia. In the middle of a harsh Patagonian winter, the radio was not working and one of his workers, named Olave, went to the nearest Estancia to ask for help. It took him two days to get there and by the time help arrived at the Estancia Cristina, it was too late.

Herbert Masters and guests.
Source: Estancia Cristina Sociedad Anónima.

The passing of Herbertleft Janet as the last member of the Masters family.

Gradually, the ranch began to adopt the conditions set by Parks and removed several of its sheep. Some of the sheep were sold and others were used to pay wages. Shearing ceased to exist.

Janet spent the summers at the Estancia and the winters in Rio Gallegos; she had the company of numerous dogs who decorated the place and welcomed visitors with affection.

As a recipient of an art magazine, Janet eventually developed her skills as a painter. Some of her paintings show her beloved dogs.

With the help of a group of climbers and friends, Janet remodeled the main house, built rooms and set up a small lodge in the estancia, trying to comply with the condition of Parks that requested to turn to the tourist activity that catered to private guides and also regular hikers who came to the area, Janet would spend long hours chatting with many of these visitors who would pleasantly write her letters thanking her for her hospitality, thus being able to build this story of the last years of the Estancia already in a more touristy stage.

Janet Masters and her pets.
Source: Estancia Cristina Sociedad Anónima.

This was the way it worked until 1997, when Janet died at the age of 93. The land of Estancia Cristina is since then under the direct control of Los Glaciares National Park.

But what could the Park do with a place that had won the hearts of every visitor who came to its shores?

The reconversion of Estancia Cristina

The National Parks Administration decided to give the facilities of Estancia Cristina in concession to a private company that would be in charge of exploiting it for tourism and that would maintain a friendly treatment and develop environmentally sustainable activities. This has been the case since 2001, and the concessions have been adapted to accommodate the tourists who arrive here, as always, by boat.

Estancia Cristina accepts a limited number of visitors per day, it also has twenty high standard rooms to accommodate visitors to this paradise. It functions as a fishing lodge; fishing enthusiasts must obtain a special permit from the National Park and be accompanied by a licensed guide in order to fish for the Chinook salmon found in the Caterina River.

But above all you can discover the history of this place and the history of Patagonia in its historic buildings and sheds, reliving the journey of the Masters family: a family that came with dreams and left a small mark on the infinite Patagonia.

Last words

This is the end of our journey and I wanted to end here because this last story should be an inspiration for the whole region.

Today, because of the late failure of the sheep-farming culture, Patagonia seems empty. And it gives us the feeling that it will never change. So it feels that the history of Patagonia was written and that is it. We assume that Patagonia is already tagged for life but I believe differently.

Due to the latest achievements of the young community of the region, you can see they are trying to protect their homes: in the last years, a large community stood up against the dams on the Santa Cruz River and they are trying so hard to stop its construction. In Chubut, the government wanted to extract gold through mega mining companies that could potentially poison the water, but the population stood up, too. Bright times are coming. Maybe Patagonia can be reconverted and in the next 200 years we can see this region thriving again, and hopefully for good.

CONCLUSION

You will have realized that there is much that is unknown about Patagonia. It is taken for granted that there were some transcendental historical facts that are an unavoidable part of it; but in this work I invited you to review some other aspectsas well.

The accounts of the explorers of yesteryear were wedded to religious faith and from that angle they viewed the native peoples of Patagonia with misfortune, fear and disgust. This can be seen in the opinions they left on record, including even Darwin. Historians of the early twentieth century endorsed the acts of violence that took place in the unfortunate genocides of Patagonia in support of an Argentine government perpetuated by electoral fraud.

With immigration and the arrival of different groups of settlers, the Patagonian soil was democratized, although there were some people who took advantage of the bonanza situation. They bent the rules in their favor and enriched themselves in such a treacherous way that even the national authorities depended on them. This situation of dependence would end up tilting the modern destiny of Patagonia.

At the moment in history when the scales could have been balanced, I am talking about the Patagonian strikes, it was the national authorities who ended up defending the interests of their patrons (big landowners), leaving aside the interests of the new citizens of Patagonia, whom they treated mercilessly, being accomplices of injustice.

The writers of the rest of the 20th century speak of a Patagonian progress boosted by the estancias, and the "pioneer" families. But they always forget to mention these aberrant facts that were silenced for years and years. The arrival of Osvaldo Bayer as a historian is what began to open this path of revisionism with his work "*La Patagonia Rebelde*". With the publication of this book, it is beginning to be noticed that more opinions contrary to the official history told up to that moment are coming to light. But many writers still decide to deal very casually with these aberrant chapters.

Sometimes I think that some writers dodge the truth in order not to hurt susceptibilities. Or they give another name to the facts to exorcise their friends from any guilt that may befall them.

My wish is that the story can be balanced one day.

In this book, I compiled the facts, and named things as they plainly appear to me. The truth should not embarrass anyone, but should teach us not to make the same mistakes over again. Towards the end of the book, I try to get out of the monotony of sheep farming and agriculture to explore other facets of the region such as its natural resources.

The richness of this area is incalculable. Where we had solitude, communication appeared and telegraph and telephone lines, mail and land transportation arrived. The mountains began to interact with humans. The romance between nature and human began again. We established the relationship between Patagonia and Antarctica, two distant cousins who find in their cold solitude a bond that brings them closer. Others who have a great bond are Chileans and Argentines. Unfortunately, we are still living in the past: we like to reopen wounds, blame, and live in conflict. But we have an enormous potential to work as a team and to be able to rethink Patagonia for what it can still be.

To conclude, the Masters family lived in isolation and still managed to move forward with their family project. They adapted to the situations that surrounded them and, when sheep farming no longer had a place, they were able to reconvert and adapt to the new paradigm in which they found themselves. And I think this is an example to keep in mind at this moment and ask ourselves: Where do we Patagonians stand?

We are still few, and we need a lot of support from the governmental structure to continue developing the few cities that exist in such an extensive territory. In other words, we are still dependent. And dependence does not allow us to see anything in the long term. How good it would be to be able to reach a point were the region has enough autonomy to decide what is best for its future. The people of Patagonia do not need someone to come to extract gold in Chubut or to install a dam on the Santa Cruz River because a foreign power decided to invest in the country.

Patagonians need to be able to identify themselves with their place, to vindicate their culture, their native peoples, to embrace their history, to understand it, and to feel that they really own the place.

The Patagonian people should feel proud of where they are: they are there by choice, by conviction, or by inheritance.

I think the main message I want to send is that Patagonia should not only be the result of what happened a few centuries ago.

Yes, today we see the result of these historical processes, but it should not be definitive. We must keep in mind that history is written day by day and that what we do today will have an impact on the time to come. We usually show travelers the most beautiful landscapes, but Patagonia can be so much more.

It seems that sheep farming was the past, and that, due to its current conditions, it is a resource that, with many doubts, could be rebounding again. Without sheep farming, space and emptiness become endless.

We continue to extract minerals, but I don't know how much longer it will be a lasting employment with all the issues surrounding energy. Fishing has potential, but no control. Tourism continues to be one of the most sustainable economic options, but it is not enough to move the region forward.

With the pandemic, we have noticed how much the communities that live from tourism are suffering. That is why it is important to look for a change, a reconversion in the way of thinking about life in Patagonia. Do we want to continue depending on the contexts or do we want to look for a structure that allows the region to empower itself and be self-sufficient. It is time to write a new history in the region.

Patagonia was the native peoples, the Estancia, the sheep, the hard work and the loneliness. That is our past, for better or worse. Now we have so much more: youth, identity, energy, more rights, more information, natural resources, new National Parks, media, and best of all: a vast territory where the potential is infinite.

Learning from our past, to manage the present with wisdom. That must be the future of Patagonia.

Juan Manuel Herrera Traybel

Thank you for reading this book.

If you liked it, I'd be happy if you recommended it to your friends. I would also appreciate it if you would leave a review on Amazon or Goodreads. It's the best way for my book to be seen and vouched for.

ABOUT THE AUTHOR

Juan Manuel Herrera Traybel was born in Buenos Aires in 1987.

His interest in Patagonia began when, at the age of seventeen, he first encountered the region. Amazed by his encounter with the snow and the mountains, he took the images with him and kept them in his mind.

Without knowing what his future held for him, he began to study tourism. In his first year of study and thanks to his proficiency in English, he gets the chance to do an internship at Estancia Harberton, in Tierra del Fuego. He fell in love with the experience of living in Patagonia and returned to Tierra del Fuego once again.

Continuing his education, he adds Italian and Portuguese to his repertoire of languages. After finishing his studies, he decides to travel the world, living in Australia and New Zealand for a couple years where he perfects his English.

After visiting all the continents in three years of travelling, he returns once again to Patagonia where he is licensed as a National Parks guide. There he begins a working relationship with Estancia Cristina in Los Glaciares National Park, on the shores of Lago Argentino.

Captivated by the history of the place, he presents a project to improve the state of the Museum of the place with the aim of raising awareness of the company to protect the heritage of the place and, in turn, improve the experience of visitors. Supported by the concession company and his co-workers, he is carrying out a two-year research project. What started with curiosity turned into a work of historical study deep enough to be able to understand the history of a family and all the historical contexts that took place in the Patagonian region.

Thanks to this last experience, Herrera became a Patagonian history enthusiast and curator of the Estancia Cristina Museum. He now lives in Austria, where, in the wake of the coronavirus pandemic, he began to outline this book project and after more two years of silent work, he delivers us this independent historical work.

BIBLIOGRAPHY

- Shipton, E. (2013) Tierra de Tempestades. Editorial Sudpol – Buenos Aires. Argentina.
- Vairo, C. (1995) Los Yámana. Zagier & Urruty Publications - Buenos Aires, Argentina.
- Ygobone, A. (1950) Paladines Auténticos de la Patagonia. Editorial El Ateneo - Buenos Aires, Argentina.
- Halvorsen, P. (1997) Entre el Río de las Vueltas y los Hielos Continentales. Editorial Vinciguerra - Buenos Aires, Argentina.
- Borrero, J. (1928) La Patagonia Trágica. Los Yámana. Zagier & Urruty Publications - Buenos Aires, Argentina.
- Guzmán, Y. (2009) Viejas Estancias de la Patagonia. Editorial Claridad. Buenos Aires, Argentina.
- Borrero, L. (2001) El poblamiento de la Patagonia. Emecé Editores - Buenos Aires, Argentina.
- Alonso, M (1993) Manual del Lago Argentino y Glaciar Perito Moreno. Zagier & Urruty Publications - Buenos Aires, Argentina.
- Vairo, C. y Gutti, F. (2000) Oro en Tierra del Fuego! Zagier & Urruty Publications - Buenos Aires, Argentina.
- Capdevila, R. (2000) Antártida. Zagier & Urruty Publications - Buenos Aires, Argentina.
- Vairo, C (2007) Antártida: asentamientos balleneros históricos. Zagier & Urruty Publications - Buenos Aires, Argentina
- Acuña, H (2015) Diario del Estafeta. Asociación Civil Museo Marítimo de Ushuaia. Tierra del Fuego, Argentina.
- Vairo, C. (1997) Isla de los Estados y Faro del Fin del Mundo. Buenos Aires, Argentina.
- Canclini, A. (2008) Darwin y los Fueguinos. Zagier & Urruty Publications - Buenos Aires, Argentina
- Dobreé, P. (2006) El Gran Arreo. Zagier & Urruty Publications - Buenos Aires, Argentina
- Prichard, H. (1902) Through the Heart of Patagonia. D. Appleton & Co. - New York, USA.
- Baliña, M. y Von der Fetch, F. (2016) A orillas del Lago Argentino. Photo Design Ediciones- Buenos Aires, Argentina.
- Onelli, C. (1930) Trepando los Andes. El Elefante Blanco Ediciones - Buenos Aires, Argentina.

- Matthews, A. (2004) Crónica de la colonia galesa de la Patagonia. Ediciones Alfonsina - Buenos Aires, Argentina.
- Basanta, A. (2013) El correo argentino en Patagonia. Patagonia Sur Libros - Buenos Aires, Argentina.
- Goodall, N. (1979) Tierra del Fuego. Ediciones Shanamaiim – Tierra del Fuego, Argentina.
- Luna, F. (1988) La inmigración. Editorial Abril -Buenos Aires, Argentina.
- Ripa, J. (1987) Inmigrantes en la Patagonia. Marymar Ediciones - Buenos Aires, Argentina.
- Alonso Marchante, L. (2014) Menéndez, Rey de la Patagonia. Editorial Catalonia, Santiago de Chile, Chile.
- Bayer, O. (2015) La Patagonia Rebelde. Editorial Planeta - Buenos Aires, Argentina.